YORK NOTE

General Editors: Professor A.N.
of Stirling) & Professor Suheil
University of Beirut)

William Wycherley

THE COUNTRY WIFE

Notes by Christopher Murray

MA (NUI) PH D (YALE)
Statutory Lecturer in English Literature,
University College, Dublin

LONGMAN
YORK PRESS

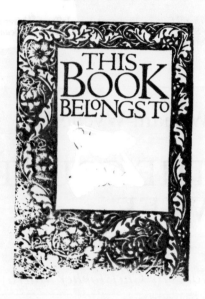

YORK PRESS
Immeuble Esseily, Place Riad Solh, Beirut.

LONGMAN GROUP UK LIMITED
Longman House,
Burnt Mill,
Harlow,
Essex

First published 1987

ISBN 0-582-95704-4

Produced by Longman Group (FE) Ltd
Printed in Hong Kong

Contents

Part 1

Introduction

The life and works of William Wycherley

William Wycherley, eldest son of a Shropshire lawyer, was born about 28 March 1641* in Clive, near Shrewsbury, Shropshire. When he was about fifteen years of age he was sent to study in France, where he came into contact with the latest French literary ideas. In particular, the future playwright was exposed to the new ideas on comedy and theatrical entertainment then beginning to flourish in France, which were soon destined to find fresh growth in England after the king, Charles II (1630–85), returned there in 1660 after his forced exile. In France Wycherley became a Roman Catholic. After his return to England, in about 1659, he reverted to Protestantism, and decided to follow his father's profession as a lawyer. He was admitted to the Inner Temple, one of the training colleges for lawyers in London, on 10 November 1659, but soon forsook law for the life of a Restoration playwright. Wycherley may at some time in the 1660s have served in the navy, as he wrote a poem entitled 'On a Sea Fight which the Author was in, betwixt the English and the Dutch'.

London after 1660 was an exciting and a lively place for a young author to be. Following the end of the Commonwealth (1642–60) there was a spirit of release and celebration in England. Puritan repression of literature and theatre was at an end. Pleasure was no longer a sin. New theatres were built, and the king himself became a patron of dramatic entertainments, thereby sanctioning them and lending them official approval. This royal approval made an extraordinary difference to the general artistic atmosphere. After all, if Charles let it be known that he regarded wit and pleasure as two of the desirable pursuits in life, then these were sought after and became the values of the age. Charles also indicated by his interest in the actresses (see below) – especially in Nell Gwynn (1650–87) – that he regarded time spent in the theatres as time well spent. This attitude was bound to encourage writers, performers and members of the audience to flock to the theatres too, as places of fashionable rendezvous. Wycherley was simply one of the many who flocked there.

* See Arthur Friedman (ed.), *The Plays of William Wycherley*, Clarendon Press, Oxford, 1979, p.xiii and note 3, for a discussion of Wycherley's date of birth.

The order in which Wycherley wrote his four comedies is not known for certain. He himself claimed that he wrote *Love in a Wood* at the age of nineteen, *The Gentleman Dancing-Master* at twenty-one, *The Plain Dealer* at twenty-five, and *The Country Wife* at thirty-two. It seems unlikely that these dates are true, because *Love in a Wood* was not staged until about March 1671, when Wycherley was thirty, and the other plays followed. But it is at least possible that the order is correct here, and that *The Plain Dealer* was written before *The Country Wife*, even though it was staged after it. This would mean that *The Country Wife* was Wycherley's most mature play – it is certainly his best.

Love in a Wood, or, St. James's Park serves notice that this new playwright was going to continue the 'comedy of wit' rendered popular by writers of the 1660s, such as John Dryden (1631–1700). Broadly speaking, the leading features of this sort of comedy were as follows:

(1) a love story with two pairs of sophisticated, witty lovers;
(2) a location in London, with specific settings in fashionable places, such as St. James's Park;
(3) a male character who seems more interested in sex than in marriage, known as the rake-hero;
(4) a desirable heroine, possessed of a fortune, who engages the rake-hero in a battle of wits;
(5) at least one foolish older woman, desperately disguising sexual appetite under a pretence of respectability;
(6) several characters who are types or representative of social attitudes or mores, such as a dandy or fop, a suspicious husband, a merchant.

Love in a Wood could be called a realistic comedy, if we restrict that description here to mean a reflection of the manners or lifestyle of Wycherley's contemporaries. He was, like many playwrights of his time, holding the mirror up to society, at least to upper-class society. But Wycherley was slightly less good-humoured than others about what he saw around him, the values by which people were living. He liked to prick holes in the fabric of public morality. For example, he has a character in his first play called Lady Flippant who wants a husband but who pretends that 'honour' is a prior concern to her. She uses the word so often that we recognise that the lady 'doth protest too much'. Here Wycherley is satirising a certain type of well-bred lady with double standards. He saw people as wearing a mask (which some literally did outdoors or at the theatre) and he wanted to show how this assumption of pretending to be good or elegant or cool could also be a disguise of natural instincts. He was not mocking Lady Flippant's sexual appetite, merely her dishonesty in not openly acknowledging it. Thus part of Wycherley's originality, part of what he had to say, lay in his observation of the contradictions by which people, probably unconsciously, live. Bringing that sort of contradiction to the surface reveals to an audience something about human nature, especially in a sophisticated society where norms of behaviour tend to merge into fashionable postures. Wycherley could go beyond this sort of analysis, however, to observation of a peculiarly devastating kind, condemning the very bases of contemporary values.

Wit and the reputation for wit were such values. Everybody wanted to be able to turn an elegant phrase, engage in repartee, throw off a line or two which others might quote in the coffee-houses; the young men who fancied themselves as experts in this area were known as town wits (Wycherley was one himself). But in *Love in a Wood* a character says: 'What are wits but contemners [despisers] of matrons, seducers, or defamers of married women, and deflowerers of helpless virgins, even in the streets' (III.1.54–8). This brings the fashionable gentleman down to earth with a bump. This levelling quality ('what are they ... but') is part of Wycherley's very acute comic style. He was critical and judgemental.

Obviously, the first audiences of *Love in a Wood* liked Wycherley's style. We read that 'His Company was not only courted by the Men, but his Person was as well received by the LADIES; and as K. CHARLES was extremely *Fond* of him upon account of his *Wit*, some of the Royal Mistresses ... set *no less Value* upon *Those Parts* in him, of which they were more proper Judges'.* It was a naughty age. Wycherley both enjoyed it and criticised it. One of the said ladies formerly beloved by King Charles, Lady Castlemaine, became Wycherley's lover. On one occasion she shouted bawdily at him from her carriage in the street and he, from his carriage, asked her if she would be at the theatre that night, adding that if she were he would see her even though he would be breaking a date with another woman. To do that, she agreed, would be to disappoint a woman who had favoured him for one who had not. Ah yes, was Wycherley's response, but the woman who had *not* favoured him was the finer of the two, and he who would be constant to Lady Castlemaine until he could find a finer, was sure to die her slave. She blushed, and told her coachman to drive on. That night she was in the king's box at Drury Lane Theatre and Wycherley was in the pit below her, from where he talked to her during the whole play (it cannot have been his own!). And this began a love affair which made, as they say, a great noise in the town. This episode reveals a significant point: that there was a very thin line at this time between drama and life. The dialogue that took place in the street between Lady

---

* Richard Pack, 'Memoirs of Mr. Wycherley's Life' (1728), quoted by David Cook and John Swannell, Introduction to *The Country Wife*, Methuen (Revels Plays), London, 1975, p.xix.

Castlemaine and Wycherley was just the sort of witty exchange that one would expect in a play. And the love affair was born in the theatre itself, while she sat in the royal box. We can guess that the audience were watching the flirtation as eagerly (and maybe more eagerly) than the play itself. This is worth bearing in mind when we come to study *The Country Wife*: what happens on stage is deliberately close, in speech and in behaviour, to what went on in polite society.

After this time, everything Wycherley wrote was of absorbing interest to the town, since, it was felt, his work must in some way reflect the goings-on of the 'in' circle, the centre of which was the king himself. But his next play, *The Gentleman Dancing-Master*, staged by the Duke's Company in 1672, was a disappointment and Wycherley wisely waited three years before trying again, with *The Country Wife*, first performed on 12 January 1675 at the new Theatre Royal in Drury Lane. With this outrageous play, daring even by the loose moral standards of the day, Wycherley reached the pinnacle of his success. He followed it up with *The Plain Dealer*, staged in December 1676 at Drury Lane, where it became abundantly clear that Wycherley wasn't just mirroring the loose living of the age but attacking it too. This hard-hitting play has for its hero Captain Manly, the 'plain dealer' who always speaks his mind instead of indulging in the hypocritical politeness of the day. Wycherley himself was hereafter known as 'Manly', in recognition of his outspoken honesty about society.

Although he was only in his mid-thirties, Wycherley wrote no more plays after *The Plain Dealer*. He fell into bad health, during which time King Charles supported him. On his recovery Wycherley met and married Lady Drogheda in 1679 and King Charles was so annoyed by the secretive way in which the marriage was arranged that he withdrew his patronage from Wycherley. This shows how close Wycherley had previously been to the king. When Lady Drogheda died in 1681 Wycherley became involved in an expensive lawsuit which landed him in debtors' prison, some say for seven years. It was Charles's successor, King James II (1633–1701), who paid off Wycherley's debts and set him free. He also granted him a pension. But James did not last long on the throne, for he was driven off it by his son-in-law William of Orange (1650–1702) in 1688, and when that happened Wycherley lost royal patronage. King William was no friend to the theatres. The golden days of Restoration theatre were drawing to a close, as a reaction began to set in against the so-called immorality and profaneness of the stage.

Restoration comedy reached its final flowering in the plays of William Congreve (1670–1729) and George Farquhar (1678–1707) but by now Wycherley had nothing to do with the theatre. Instead he concentrated on writing poetry, and on the art of conversation. In 1704 his *Miscellany Poems* were published but were unenthusiastically received.

It was common for writers at this time to think that plays were less valuable as literature than almost any other kind of composition, with the result that many playwrights tried to achieve what they hoped was lasting fame by forms other than drama. It is an odd irony that their fame, after all, was to hinge on their plays. Wycherley was, however, to impress the young poet Alexander Pope (1688–1744) with his volume of poems, and Pope became a kind of secretary and tidier-up of Wycherley's unpublished writings for a time. Eventually, in 1729, Pope published a collection entitled *The Posthumous Works of William Wycherley, Esq., In Prose and Verse*, which included the correspondence between Wycherley and himself. By now Wycherley had been dead almost fifteen years; he died on 31 December 1715, and was buried in St Paul's Church, Covent Garden.

Before he died he was put through one more incident that might have come out of one of his own plays. He was courted by a widow, Elizabeth Jackson, even while he lay sick in bed. She, however, was simply the screen for her lover, one Captain Thomas Shrimpton, who had his eye on Wycherley's money. There was a nephew, who in the normal course of events would have inherited Wycherley's estate. Captain Shrimpton was determined this would not happen, so he brought about a marriage between Elizabeth Jackson and the dying Wycherley. She then inherited the estate, which the nephew failed to recover through the law courts, and, of course, she married Captain Shrimpton. This brought to a rather comic end the life and fortunes of William Wycherley.

The theatre of the Restoration

After 1660, with the 'Restoration' of Charles II to the throne of England (hence the name of this period), theatre became both a social centre and a means of focusing and defining the values and behaviour of the age. Above all, the theatres were centres of pleasure, and we can have no real appreciation of Restoration comedy unless we accept that, for a limited period, roughly between 1660 and 1700, comedy was entirely liberated from the anxiety of moral improvement it has so often had to carry in the theatres of other ages. Because the theatre itself, as a physical structure, was such a vital source not only of entertainment but of fashionable display or style during the Restoration period it is necessary to know something of its nature and conditions at that time.

If the reader is coming to study Restoration theatre armed with ideas gained from the reading of Elizabethan drama he or she must realise that there are fundamental differences between the two kinds. The Elizabethan public theatre was in the round; in other words there was an open or thrust stage projecting well into the area where members of the audience stood, with the result that they surrounded it on three sides.

Galleries seating other members of the audience and rooms above the stage completed the circular or hexagonal shape of the wooden building. The stage was for the most part bare: there was no painted scenery and no front curtain. The actors were boys and men; no women appeared on stage. Plays were acted in the open air, using natural light. There were also private theatres, where conditions differed somewhat, but by-and-large the Elizabethan theatre can fairly be said to have possessed the features listed above. What they imply are as follows: (i) there was a large, open-air place where all sorts of people convened, with many from the poorer classes; (ii) the style of production provided could not have been realistic in view of the bare stage and the absence of actresses; it was, indeed, more symbolic than realistic; (iii) the relationship of audience to play was intimate and involved, as there was no gap between them.

The Restoration theatre was born in France, and was modelled on the form of the 'real' tennis court; that is, a rectangular building with roughly the dimensions of a tennis court, covered over and with a stage at one end, the audience seated in front, in the pit, and on three sides in boxes, and a gallery. Changeable scenery, that is to say scenery painted on large flat, moveable surfaces, was used for the first time as background. Actresses appeared on the stage. Artificial lighting was used, though the plays still took place in the afternoon as they had in Elizabethan times. We have here the beginnings of the modern stage. The implications of these changes are as follows. (i) A smaller, more class-conscious theatre. It was an elitist theatre, frequented more by the idle rich than by the poor. (ii) Once the play was divided off from the audience and perspective scenery was introduced, the possibilities for realism were created. In comedy, especially, using prose as its medium, realism became increasingly the aim. London life was mirrored on the stage. (iii) With the regular appearance of actresses, many of whom were mistresses of the playwrights themselves or of the king and his court, a sexual emphasis not possible in the drama of Shakespeare's day became commonplace. The physical presence and social reputation of these actresses gave a special tone and style to the drama, especially, once again, to comedy, which always imitates man's lower rather than his higher nature. (iv) Because of the atmosphere and conditions of the Restoration theatre, where people came to be seen rather than necessarily to watch the play, the audience tended to be somewhat detached from the comedies on stage. A critical attitude was thereby fostered, and this suggests how the modern reader should approach a Restoration comedy: as a piece of realism, a mirror of London life in the age of the Merry Monarch, to be looked at sceptically and objectively. The Restoration theatre was a cool medium.

A few further details are necessary for the proper understanding of a comedy set in Restoration times. Most of the acting was done on an apron stage or fore-stage, behind which was the changeable scenery. The actors used the stage doors, two to the left and two to the right of the stage, as entrances and exits and as doors within the play itself. In a play such as *The Country Wife*, where there is a lot of chasing of women in and out of doors which are sometimes locked, such details assume importance (see IV.3 or V.1). We must not imagine a totally realistic stage setting: a lot of fun is created out of a basic simplicity, a platform, a table and chairs, the stage doors, and a background setting to indicate the location. There is much scope in *The Country Wife* for split-second timing, as characters dart in and out of the way of unwelcome company, and part of the joy of the play lies in this theatricality, this display of inventiveness and quick response on the part of those on stage. It is also worth bearing in mind that the Restoration was an age of great actors and actresses. They found in comedies such as Wycherley's much scope for the art of calculated pretence: for the first time they had the challenge of playing ordinary men and women seeming to be leading the lives of city dwellers in quest of love, pleasure and money and yet they had the task of revealing, beneath the realism, the vanity, foolishness and self-deception of some of these city dwellers. We need to remind ourselves while we read *The Country Wife* that it is *not* real; that it is all but an invitation to performers to perform. If we bear that in mind, that there is a lot of 'acting' within the play, we stand a better chance of beginning to understand the art that lies behind the seeming effortlessness of *The Country Wife*, and the nature of the imitation which it is, amusingly, presenting with great style and elegance.

A note on the source of *The Country Wife*

Wycherley himself claimed that he wrote *The Country Wife* when he was thirty-one or thirty-two years of age, and this would put the date of composition at 1671 or 1672. It was first staged, at the new Theatre Royal in Drury Lane, on 12 January 1675, and was published in London in the same year.

One source of the play was *The Eunuch*, a classical play, in Latin, by the Roman playwright Terence (?185–159BC). This comedy is about a young lover pretending to be sexually impotent, so as to gain access to the household of the girl he loves. In that basic situation only, Wycherley's play is indebted to *The Eunuch*. Otherwise the comedies are quite different, especially in characterisation and in tone. Horner is, quite simply, a Restoration man, a modern man one might say, who has no counterpart in Terence. Another influence was the French playwright Jean-Baptiste Poquelin, usually known simply as Molière (1622–73).

His style of comedy, influenced by Italian *commedia dell' arte*, has a certain amount in common with English Restoration comedy. In general, Molière's use of farcical situations, lovers in disguise, eccentric characters, and easy, conversational dialogue, coincided closely with the tastes (formed in France) of English theatre cultivated by English Restoration playwrights from John Dryden to William Congreve. In particular, Wycherley borrowed from two of Molière's plays for *The Country Wife*, namely, the *School for Husbands* (1661) and the *School for Wives* (1662). The main situation influenced here is the attempt by Pinchwife to go to such lengths to protect his wife from men that he locks her up, and yet he ends up foolishly bringing her (although he does not realise this) to the very man he fears most, namely Horner. Pinchwife's interrogation of Margery (in IV.2) about what Horner did to her, is also indebted to Molière's the *School for Wives*. Several other little details (such as Margery's letter to Horner) can also be traced to one or other of Molière's plays. But it would be a mistake to conclude from all of this that Wycherley merely imitated Molière. *He took from Molière incidents and situations, but he gave them a setting, a tone and a basis in characterisation which were all his own.* This sort of thing is easily said, perhaps; but it can easily be tested if the reader opens a page or two of Molière (in translation, even) and then switches to Wycherley. It's like moving from innocent, childlike fun to deadly earnest. *The Country Wife* is stamped with a view of mankind and of society which is cruder and nastier than anything in Molière. It absorbs Molière's influence and transforms it into something new and original.

For details about current editions of the text please turn to the section on 'The Text' in 'Suggestions for further reading', page 63. Since line references vary from edition to edition the reader should be aware that these Notes refer to the New Mermaids edition of *The Country Wife*, edited by John Dixon Hunt, Ernest Benn, London, 1973. (Reprinted A. & C. Black, London, 1985.)

Part 2

Summaries
of THE COUNTRY WIFE

A general summary

Horner, a young man of fashion, has put the story around London by means of a doctor, his friend Quack, that he has become impotent following a trip to France. His purpose is to attract women to him, and he believes that this trick will, paradoxically, achieve that aim. The play then proceeds to prove him right. Sir Jasper Fidget, a businessman, seeks out Horner to be the companion of his wife, Lady Fidget, his sister, Dainty Fidget, and their friend Mistress Squeamish. He wishes to pursue his own affairs as a businessman, and considers that the ladies will be safe in Horner's care. Horner, of course, eventually seduces all three of the ladies.

A second story involves Pinchwife, a middle-aged and jealous man recently married to a country girl, Margery. She is the 'country wife' of the title. Pinchwife is worried that Margery will be seduced by some young man in London, and he shuts her up in his house accordingly. He is particularly suspicious of Horner, whom he knows to be just the sort of woman-chaser he himself used to be. It is important for the plot that Pinchwife is not aware of Horner's claim to be impotent. Thus when Horner shows an interest in Margery, Pinchwife goes to excessive lengths to warn her against him and against the various evils of the town. The result is that he only arouses her curiosity. Meanwhile, in a third plot, Pinchwife's sister Alithea is supposed to marry Sparkish, a foolish dandy or fop. In fact, the only reason Pinchwife is in London at all, with his country wife, is for the wedding of Alithea to Sparkish, after which he intends to get back to the safety of the country as quickly as possible. But Alithea meets Harcourt, a friend of Horner's, and they fall in love. She is too moral to drop Sparkish, however, on the day before her wedding. Harcourt disguises himself as a parson and pretends to marry Alithea to Sparkish. Since this is not a real marriage ceremony Alithea is free to marry Harcourt, when she comes to see how undeserving Sparkish really is.

The three plots are very skilfully interwoven in the play. Margery Pinchwife, disguised as Alithea, is sent by Pinchwife to Horner. Pinchwife actually thinks he is sending his sister, and he does this rather than risk Horner getting at his wife. Horner is greatly surprised at this sudden gift, and loses no time in getting better acquainted with Margery.

But when Pinchwife tells Sparkish that Alithea has gone by her own choice to be Horner's lover, Sparkish goes to her and attacks her publicly for walking out on him. Concerned about her good name, Alithea then goes to Horner's lodgings, accompanied by Pinchwife and Harcourt. Meanwhile, Horner has had an assignation at his lodgings with Lady Fidget, who, although insisting she is a woman of honour, is quite willing to be his lover, so long as he is discreet. The famous 'china' scene occurs here, as Sir Jasper interrupts the assignation and Lady Fidget pretends she was collecting china. A little later, Lady Fidget and her two women friends, Dainty Fidget and Mrs Squeamish, interrupt Horner's love-making with Margery. She goes into hiding, and they start to drink and confess their real natures. Soon after this, Alithea arrives to question Horner about the slander on her good name. To her horror Horner insists that the story is true, that he has had sex with her. He says this so as to protect Margery, who is still hiding. Harcourt is about to challenge Horner to a duel when Margery runs out of hiding, worried for Horner's safety. Alithea is shown to be innocent, by Margery's actions and the confession of Alithea's maid, Lucy. Just then Sir Jasper Fidget, Lady Fidget and the other ladies come in and prevent Pinchwife from doing violence to Margery. They tell him that he need not worry, because Horner is impotent. Margery is about to blurt out that to her certain knowledge this isn't so, when the other ladies force her to stay quiet. Reluctantly, Pinchwife believes the story and excuses Margery. After the assurance that Alithea and Harcourt are to be married, the play ends with the women keeping Horner's secret.

Detailed summaries

Prologue, spoken by Master Hart

Playwrights, like thugs, never give in just because they get a punch or two, but will persist until you yourself are tired out punching. So it is with the writer before you today, whose last play you attacked: he asks me to persist and challenge the audience with this prologue to his new play. But I myself, as an actor, am not too happy about confronting you like this, although I've often been tough enough on stage. I'd rather make my peace with you, in spite of what the author says behind the scenes. Besides, as you know, we actors are often on your side and murder the poor playwright on the stage. In fact, so much are we on your side that we throw open the backstage area to you, and when you come backstage we let you do your worst to the writers and cast, not excluding the actresses.

NOTES AND GLOSSARY:

Master Hart: the actor Charles Hart (died 1683) was one of the best-known actors on the Restoration stage. He was famous for playing Brutus in Shakespeare's *Julius Caesar* and Othello in Shakespeare's play of that name. He also distinguished himself in comedies. He played the leading role in three of Wycherley's plays, including that of Horner in *The Country Wife*

late so baffled scribbler: Wycherley himself, whose second play, *The Gentleman Dancing-Master*, had been something of a flop three years earlier, in 1672

first draw on you: draw swords, like cowards who would pretend courage by being the first to challenge somebody

still pit: the pit was the parterre or the area of the auditorium now known as the stalls. Wycherley is suggesting that he is uncertain of his reception

Kastril: a character in *The Alchemist* (1610), a comedy by Ben Jonson (1572–1637), who was always quarrelling

give the lie: accuse someone of lying. To do this before the other person has even spoken is obviously to provoke an argument

Bayes's battle: the battle on behalf of the poets. A crown of bay or laurel was traditionally placed on the poet's brow. Below, line 16, Bayes stands for Wycherley

confederate wits . . . no quarter: an example of Wycherley's flattering the audience, who would like to be thought of as 'wits' or clever men-about-town. 'Confederate' means in union, marshalled as for battle. Hence the military usage, 'no quarter': no mercy

huffing: bullying

tiring-room: dressing-room

give up to you/Our poets, virgins: the speaker continues the military metaphor, as if to say, 'we, weak enemy, surrender all to you'

Act 1 Scene 1

Horner meets his friend, a doctor named Quack, who àssures him he has spread the story around London that Horner, lately returned from France, has had a venereal disease which has left him impotent. Quack wonders what the idea behind this is, and when Horner explains that it is to gain him new lovers, he doubts if the plan will work. Just then they are visited by Sir Jasper Fidget, who comes to gloat over Horner's impotence; his wife Lady Fidget accompanies him, together with his sister Mistress Dainty Fidget. Horner is deliberately insulting to the ladies, as if he could not stand the sight of them. They, in turn, seem disgusted by him, and Sir Jasper is highly amused. He invites Horner to visit his house and play cards with the ladies. Then he goes off to his business interests elsewhere, taking the ladies with him. Quack thinks that Horner has just shown how useless his plan is. Horner points out that Sir Jasper has in fact invited him to be his wife's escort. He sees several other advantages to the rumour of his sexual status, mainly that it will reveal by their distaste of his condition those women who are in fact interested in sex, and then all he has to do to have them is to assure them of his healthy state.

Horner is joined by Harcourt and Dorilant, two of his friends, who are not aware of the truth behind his supposed impotence. He pretends to be quite hostile to women. Sparkish comes in, a foolish dandy, who teases Horner about his condition and then goes off to meet his fiancée Alithea and bring her to the theatre to see a new play. Then Pinchwife enters, an old acquaintance of Horner's but not exactly a friend. In fact, because he has married (at the age of forty-nine) a young and pretty country wife, Pinchwife is determined that Horner shall not even see her. Pinchwife is in London only on a short visit, to attend the wedding of his sister Alithea to Sparkish. He is disturbed to hear that Horner has already seen his wife Margery at the playhouse, where Pinchwife had brought her the day before. Horner says how much he admired this girl, but Pinchwife says it was not his wife, who, he claims, is quite ugly. They tease him even more then, as if he had brought another woman to the theatre. Horner declares he was powerfully attracted to this woman, and Pinchwife leaves quickly, jealous of Horner's interest. He does not know and is not told of Horner's supposed impotence.

NOTES AND GLOSSARY:

as fit for:	suitable as. Horner means that a doctor is suited to procure a woman because, like a midwife, he serves to 'deliver'
orange-wenches:	orange-sellers, who obviously would gossip about the latest scandal
fumbling keepers:	sexually incompetent lovers of 'kept' women
tire-women:	those who help ladies to dress (attire), waiting women
Whitehall:	the royal palace in Westminster, London
great ones:	that is, 'pox' or syphilis
Aniseed Robin:	he was a seller in the streets of London, and was also a hermaphrodite

chirurgeon: surgeon
malady: syphilis
bills to disparage our medicaments: advertisements criticising our cures
compassed: achieved
discovers: reveals
cause: plea-
rooks: cheats
A pox!: a common exclamation, invoking a curse
sisters: not literally 'sisters', simply 'girls' with the suggestion that they are whores
formal: pompous
occasional: opportune, timely
acquainted: Sir Jasper means, 'won't you kiss her?' Horner insolently refuses to greet the ladies
Makes horns: that is, he puts fingers to his head in imitation of horns. As in Shakespeare's plays, references to horns always imply deceived husbands (cuckolds)
Mercury: a cure for syphilis
Ecole des Filles: (*French*) *School for Girls*, a pornographic work
chairs: a form of public transport at the time
presently: soon
innocent: harmless
abuse: (verb) deceive
duns: debt collectors
starting the game: flushing it out of hiding. The image is from hunting
right: 'game' for sexual intercourse
passe-partout: (*French*) master-key, hence one who has access everywhere
Probatum est: (*Latin*) it has been proven
you'll abroad: you'll go outdoors
as you were wont: as you used to
bear it bravely: present a confident manner
vizard-mask: whore
great-bellied: pregnant
when all's gone: when a man is impotent
boxes: at the theatre. These women would be the elegant ladies of the town
beaux garçons: (*French*) handsome fellows. Here, obviously, they are impotent
wenching: womanising
relish: improve the taste of
doze: make sleepy
he has reason: he is right

nauseous offerers of wit: sickening pretenders

cuckold's: deceived husband's

Sir Martin Mar-all: character in a play by John Dryden who mimed to music but did it badly

Your bully: the 'your' expresses a generality, not a personal possession

arrantest: most decided, worst

sparks: lively lads

signs: as for taverns and other shops

exceptious: liable to take offence

stomach: appetite

lose the new play: miss the performance, which would take place in early afternoon

mistress: fiancée, not 'mistress' in the modern sense

grumness: grimness, over-seriousness. Horner's joke is that Pinchwife must be married since he looks so miserable

cracked title: an unsound legal right; Sparkish is a 'bad bargain'

circumspection: caution

jade: horse. Smithfield was London's cattle market

foiled: defiled

clap: venereal disease

grazier: farmer

breeding: good manners. But Horner is also teasing Pinchwife by suggesting another meaning, 'pregnancy'

swinging stomachs: huge appetites

baggage: woman

honest: chaste

gamester's: gambler's

box: dice box

eighteen-penny place: the gallery in the theatre, where the cost of admission was eighteen pence. It was not among the good seats

Hampshire: a general term for 'country'

Cheapside: the area of London where the merchants lived. Most Restoration comedies made fun of merchants and 'citizens'

Act Two Scene One

Pinchwife tries to convince his wife Margery that London life, in its pleasures and pursuits, is something to be avoided. He blames his sister Alithea for telling her too much about this life, but in fact he himself tells her far more, and thereby arouses her curiosity and interest, when he warns her against various possible temptations. He also makes the mistake of telling her that a well-known libertine (Horner) admired her at the theatre the day before. When Sparkish, Alithea's fiancé, enters with his friend Harcourt Pinchwife sends Margery away quickly lest she attract the notice of Harcourt.

Pinchwife then acts as commentator on what he regards as Sparkish's foolishness in letting Harcourt pay his respects to Alithea. Indeed, urged on by Sparkish, Harcourt *does* flirt with her, and she engages in witty repartee in turn, so that we get a love scene enclosed within the opposing viewpoints of Sparkish (too dull to see what is going on) and Pinchwife (who is only too aware of the flirtation). This 'play-within-a-play' structure is a mark of Restoration comic style. In this scene Harcourt goes too far when he implies that Sparkish is 'A senseless, drivelling idiot', and Sparkish might have caused trouble at this point if Alithea had not protected Harcourt by claiming he was merely testing Sparkish's friendship. All three then leave together to go to the theatre.

Just as Pinchwife is about to see how Margery is getting on inside, Lady Fidget, Mrs Dainty Fidget and Mrs Squeamish enter to take her to the theatre also. Pinchwife pretends Margery has locked herself in her room and that she has smallpox, but his excuses are not accepted and he goes in, hoping, presumably, that the ladies will go away. They, however, have no intention of moving, and are soon joined by Sir Jasper Fidget, Horner and Dorilant. Immediately, the ladies assume a prim, easily-shocked manner, although a few minutes earlier, when left on their own, they betrayed how far from innocent they are. Sir Jasper wants the ladies to go to the theatre with Horner, since he feels it would not be proper for them to go unattended by a man and since Horner (he thinks) presents no danger. Dorilant is dismissed by Sir Jasper at this point. But Horner pretends that the last thing he wants to do is to accompany the ladies, and insults them accordingly. Sir Jasper has to beg the ladies to accept the arrangement, and has to convince Horner that accompanying and amusing the ladies is all he is fit for now. Clearly, the joke here is altogether on Sir Jasper, though he does not know it. Out of Sir Jasper's hearing, Horner explains to Lady Fidget that he is, in fact, as healthy and normal as any man, and she then pretends, as if reluctantly, to yield to Sir Jasper's wish that she make all use of Horner. Sir Jasper goes off to look after his business affairs, and Horner goes to the theatre with the three ladies.

NOTES AND GLOSSARY:

close: enclosed

the New Exchange: a place of trade, with shops and galleries

carry you: bring you

toused and moused: pulled about and manhandled

foot-post: one who carries messages on foot. Alithea is criticising Margery's unsophisticated notion of leisure. In London, as opposed to the country, people did not simply take exercise like horses

smallpox: until about 1800, when vaccination was discovered, smallpox was a much feared disease. Margery, of course, innocently calls it 'the pox' (syphilis)

fropish: peevish, cross

nangered: angered. Margery, in her unsophisticated way, often uses this kind of 'pet' talk

jill-flirt, a gadder, a magpie: a flirt, a gadabout, a chatterer

documents: instructions

chid: rebuked

basilisks: mythical creatures whose looks were supposed to kill

this easy coxcomb: this foolish dandy, that is, Sparkish

resolve me: tell me

railleurs: (*French*) mockers

Insensible: unfeeling

condole: mourn. Sparkish seems to share the cynical view that to be married is to be dead, yet he is about to get married himself

wants: lacks

earnest: pledge, advance payment

pander: pimp. (The word comes from Pandarus, who 'sold' Cressida to Troilus)

in necessity for a cloak: in need of a screen (for extra-marital affairs). It might also mean 'to hide pregnancy'

cit: citizen (regarded with contempt by the 'wits' of the day)

bubble: silly fellow, dupe

parts: talents, brains

trimmings: decorated clothes

freehold: property (his wife)

Mr Tattle or Master Limberham: apparently made-up names to suggest harmless gossips or pretenders to sexual intrigue

only by censuring others: by attacking others. Horner means that the ladies can only be thought virtuous if they constantly criticise others

arithmetical: over-precise

ombre: card game

French wether:	a wether is a castrated ram; 'French' implies diseased (sexually): thus, a eunuch
drolling:	ridiculous
we make fine:	we force (those whom we can't use as lovers) to pay money
shocks:	pet dogs
receipts:	recipes
gamester:	gambler
tailor's:	this should probably read 'tailors' (nominative case, plural). Lady Fidget means 'any more than your tailors would'
save you harmless:	keep you from harm

Act Three Scene One

Margery has now become restless, and wishes to savour the pleasures of the town. While blaming Alithea for putting ideas in her head, Pinchwife agrees to let Margery take an evening walk, disguised as her brother.

NOTES AND GLOSSARY:

pure:	grand
ostler . . . teeth:	an ostler is a groom at an inn. Some ostlers would grease a horse's teeth to prevent it from eating the food provided, and so save money
receipt-book:	a book not just of cookery recipes but of medical information also
greasy:	unpleasant (with a pun on 'greasy dishes')

Act Three Scene Two

Horner, Harcourt and Dorilant are taking a walk at the New Exchange, discussing women and love. Harcourt confesses that he loves Alithea and wonders how he will gain her love, just as Sparkish enters and reveals that he does not mind how Harcourt flirts with Alithea at the playhouse, although *she* minded. In his comments on the playhouse and his behaviour there, Sparkish once again reveals what a conceited, superficial fellow he is. When Alithea enters, along with Margery and Pinchwife on their evening walk, Sparkish hides so as not to be bothered with her. Horner watches Margery as she buys from a book-seller and follows her (without recognising her), tormenting Pinchwife by his unwelcome attention. Once Pinchwife tells the lie that this is not his wife but her brother, he cannot prevent Horner from flirting with her and even taking her away for a short time, which makes him jealous to a comical degree. Meanwhile, Harcourt has caught up with Alithea.

In the presence of the dull-witted Sparkish, Harcourt proceeds to de-
clare his love for Alithea, increasing his assault when Sparkish leaves to
attend the king's court at Whitehall. She refuses Harcourt out of
loyalty to Sparkish, and bids him goodbye for ever. Sir Jasper comes to
take Horner back to his wife and the other ladies, leaving Pinchwife
most uneasy over Horner's continuing attentions to Margery.

NOTES AND GLOSSARY:

The Scene changes: a reference which shows the new method of changeable, painted scenery. Flats were pushed on from
either side of the stage, to meet in the middle, with
a painting of the New Exchange on them

Engaged to: having an appointment with

box: at the theatre

beetle-headed: thick, stupid

lickerish: sexy

set out your hand: serve your purpose

tosses: that is, tosses dice

marker: scorekeeper

ure: use, practice

Lewis's: an (unidentified) eating-house or tavern

sack: white Spanish wine

bubbled: cheated

snack: take part, share

woodcocks: a pun on woodcock, a bird which prefers the cold
weather, and woodcock meaning a fool or one
easily 'caught' by a cheat

fond: foolish

rhyming to your Phyllis: not a real lady, but a stock name in popular
love verse

burlesque: parody, 'take-off'

hictius doctius: juggler's nonsense patter

Covent Garden Drollery: a collection of songs, poems, etc., published
in 1672. It contained one of Wycherley's own
songs, from his play *The Gentleman Dancing-
Master*

Tarugo's Wiles: a comedy by Sir Thomas St Serfe, published in
1668

The Slighted Maiden: a comedy by Sir Robert Stapylton, published in
1663

never go: 'may I never move again'. A colloquial usage

seamstresses: working in the shops in the New Exchange

power: number

proper sign: cuckold's horns

jealous:	has two meanings: either 'vehement in feeling', or 'apprehensive of evil, fearful'
eclaircissement:	(*French*) full explanation
in fine:	in short
frank:	open, outspoken
menial:	belonging to the family
canonical gentleman:	clergyman, to perform the marriage service
haunt:	annoy. Pinchwife refers here to the anxiety caused him by the 'rakehells' (ruffians), as he sees them, Horner and friends
dowdy:	an ugly woman
rubbing his forehead:	a reference to the cuckold's horns (in this play, a constant image of the husband's being deceived)
strapper:	tall and robust girl

Act Four Scene One

Lucy, Alithea's maid, tries to persuade her not to marry Sparkish, for it is the morning of their wedding, but to choose Harcourt instead. But Alithea insists that she cannot now, in honour, refuse to marry Sparkish, even though she does not love him. Lucy dismisses this scruple as nonsense. Sparkish enters with a parson, to perform the marriage ceremony, and although Alithea recognises the parson as Harcourt in clerical dress, and says so, Sparkish insists that this is Harcourt's twin brother, as he has been told so (by Harcourt himself!). They all go off to the church for the service.

NOTES AND GLOSSARY:

essence:	perfume
pulvilio:	perfumed powder
second-hand grave:	one already used
megrim:	migraine, headache
falling sickness:	epilepsy
I wish I may never stick pin more . . . gentleman:	Lucy hopes she may lose her job if she's wrong about Sparkish, whom she regards as a complete idiot ('natural') compared with Harcourt
wants:	lacks
the canonical hour:	mid-day, after which people could not get married
by the same token:	also
in a story:	in agreement
die:	a common pun, with the secondary meaning of having an orgasm

Act Four Scene Two

In their bedroom, Pinchwife roughly questions Margery about what happened in private between herself and Horner when they were alone together. What he hears makes him very jealous. He forces her to write a letter to him, clearly stating that she hates him. Unthinkingly, he tells her Horner's name and shows her how to communicate with her lover. When Pinchwife is out of the room Margery writes another letter to Horner, a love letter, and after Pinchwife returns and reads over the first letter Margery replaces it with the second and seals it up. Having locked her in her room Pinchwife goes to deliver the letter to Horner.

NOTES AND GLOSSARY:

The Scene changes to a bedchamber: again, as in III.2, painted flats would be pushed in from either side of the stage, to meet in the middle and hide the scene just used, Pinchwife's house. Notice that there are no less than four scene changes in IV

ungrateful:	disagreeable
mousled:	handled roughly
changeling:	fool
shift:	plan
y'vads:	in faith
curiously:	elegantly, skilfully
false intelligence:	wrong information (in the letter)

Act Four Scene Three

At Horner's lodging, the doctor (Quack) expresses disbelief at Horner's report on how well his plan is working. Horner places him behind a screen to observe for himself, as Lady Fidget enters. Just when she is embracing Horner her husband comes in and she pretends to be teasing Horner, to persuade him to bring her on a visit to a china shop. She then runs to Horner's room and locks herself in it, pretending to be interested in his china collection. Horner chases after her by another door, and Sir Jasper Fidget is left outside. Mrs Squeamish then enters, looking for Horner, and, hearing he is inside with Lady Fidget, enters by another door. When old Lady Squeamish, her grandmother, comes looking for her she comes out, to be followed by Lady Fidget carrying a piece of china and remarking what a lot of work it cost her to get it. There follows a double-meaning passage, where the other ladies also demand china when sex is obviously what they have in mind. Quack has no doubt about the success of Horner's scheme.

The ladies (and Sir Jasper) leave, however, when Pinchwife arrives

with the letter from Margery. Horner reads it and soon sees that Pinchwife doesn't realise it is a love letter. Nevertheless, Horner pretends not
to know what Pinchwife is talking about, thus forcing him to explain
that his wife was disguised as a boy the evening before. Horner prom-
ises to take full note of the letter. Quack is amazed when he reads the
letter for himself.

Sparkish comes in to bring Horner and Pinchwife to his wedding
feast, and Horner expresses regret that his friend (Harcourt) did not –
as he thinks – marry Alithea instead. Pinchwife reports that Alithea
has said she isn't married at all. When Pinchwife goes out, Horner per-
suades Sparkish to bring Margery to the wedding feast as well, and they
go off, as it were, to rescue her.

NOTES AND GLOSSARY:

The Scene changes to **HORNER'S** *lodging:*	two more painted flats would meet and shut off scene 2
fadges:	succeeds
projectors:	spectators, schemers
Domine:	(*Latin*) Sir
pallats:	mattresses
smocks:	women's petticoats, underclothes
squab:	short and fat
pulpit comedian:	priest. Horner is saying, in this passage, that these upright, seemingly virtuous women are all pretence, preserving a reputation for modesty by attacking playwrights' mistresses while keeping lovers themselves (priests)
chary:	careful
Machiavel:	a hypocrite. For a long time, the English popular understanding of the Italian writer Niccolò Machiavelli (1469–1527) was that he advanced hypocrisy
china:	collecting fine china was fashionable in Restoration times. This scene, known as 'the china scene', is one of the most notorious in Restoration comedy. Wycherley himself defended it in his next play, *The Plain Dealer* (II.1.)
pies and jays:	literally scavenging birds ('pies' are magpies). Here the sense is 'would-be lovers'
hackney:	for hire
tell:	count (compare 'teller' in a bank)
He is coming into you the back way:	Sir Jasper means to warn his wife that Horner is trying another door, but this is one of the very many examples of double meaning in this scene. The audience is aware, as Sir Jasper is not, that Horner is about to have sex with Lady Fidget

tomrig:	tomboy, a romping girl
viled:	vile
out of Italy with a good voice: a castrato	
toiling and moiling: working hard	
roll-wagon:	cylindrical vase
nice:	coy, fussy
diffide in:	distrust (opposite of 'confide in')
shy of:	suspicious of
Locket's:	a fashionable eating-house. A courtier would not be likely to show 'civility' to a common business-man there, unless he owed him money
Grand Signior:	Sultan of Turkey
firkin:	quarter of a barrel
dust it away:	drink quickly
pale:	fence

Act Four Scene Four

At Pinchwife's house, Margery is writing another love letter to Horner. Pinchwife comes in, and, having read the letter, grows passionately angry with her, drawing his sword and seeming about to kill her when Sparkish enters. He wants them both to join the wedding feast, but Pinchwife locks Margery in her room before going off with Sparkish.

NOTES AND GLOSSARY:

The Scene changes to PINCHWIFE'*s house*:	this was the scene used at IV.1, so the flats for IV.2 and IV.3 would now be drawn back to reveal the setting used already
distemper:	illness
dough-baked:	not baked properly, thus imperfect
politic:	natural
cully:	fool, dupe
stake:	bet. Sparkish means that the new wife will be faith-ful at first, so as to cheat more fully later on
wag:	move
sensible:	keenly felt
shy . . . of:	touchy about
comes with a fear:	occurs because people fear it
breeds for:	develops cuckold's horns

Act Five Scene One

Once again, Pinchwife cross-questions Margery about the letter she was writing to Horner at the end of Act Four. Feeling trapped, she says she wrote the letter not from herself but from Alithea, who (she says) is in love with Horner. This sounds reasonable to Pinchwife, so he believes her, but wants to see Alithea about the matter. Since, as he believes, she hasn't been properly married to Sparkish he is quite willing she should go off to Horner now, so as to protect Margery from Horner's attentions. Margery, who is learning fast how to tell lies, comes back in with the story that Alithea is so ashamed that she can't face Pinchwife, and begs to appear with her face covered, so that she can be brought to Horner's lodgings. Also, the candle must be put out. Then, after going out again briefly Margery re-enters all wrapped up and masked, pretending to be Alithea, and, thinking he has locked up Margery, Pinchwife leads her off to Horner – the very thing he was trying to avoid.

NOTES AND GLOSSARY:

A table and candle: this stage direction, like several others, suggests the realism Wycherley was attempting to convey. The candle is necessary, for the moment when Margery appears, masked, as Alithea, the candle is put out, and it is supposed to be dark (see stage direction after line 95). But in actual fact, the stage would remain bright, since plays were performed in the afternoon at this time

I resolve it: I'm making up my mind about it

Enter MRS PINCHWIFE, *masked and in hoods and scarves and a nightgown and petticoat of* ALITHEA*'s in the dark*: a stage direction that tells us a lot about the theatrical style of this play. Margery has only seconds to make the costume adjustments implied here, since she is off-stage only for eleven lines. A highly professional back-stage arrangement is clearly called for. Also, '*in the dark*' calls on the audience to imagine a darkened stage and yet to appreciate Margery's skill in manoeuvring around Pinchwife

---

Act Five Scene Two

As Quack and Horner discuss the puzzling matter of Margery's letter to Horner, Pinchwife comes in leading Margery in disguise as Alithea. Horner accepts the gift in some surprise and Pinchwife leaves. Just then Sir Jasper Fidget arrives, making Horner hide Margery away, to warn him that the ladies are about to visit Horner in masks. Horner says they must come at their peril and when Sir Jasper goes off laughing at this idle threat (as he thinks) Horner turns to his 'private feast' with Margery.

NOTES AND GLOSSARY:

The Scene changes to HORNER's *lodging*: Pinchwife's house is now blotted out by the flats painted to represent Horner's apartment

use to: are accustomed to (Quack must mean within the past day or so, since the success of Horner's plan)

cracked his credit: bankrupted himself

bit: deceived

sound: free from the pox

paw: obscene

their writings: the usurers' documents, about the loans

Act Five Scene Three

Outdoors, in Covent Garden, Pinchwife meets Sparkish and shows him the letter from, as he thinks, Alithea to Horner. Sparkish now believes that Alithea has deceived him by a pretence of love and marriage. When he meets her a moment later with her maid Lucy he attacks her fiercely for her deception. Alithea doesn't know what he's talking about, but she now sees a new side to Sparkish, that he can indeed be jealous, vindictive and cruel. So she is glad when he breaks off all relationships with her and goes off.

NOTES AND GLOSSARY:

The Scene changes to the Piazza of Covent Garden: a scene not used before in the play. Since it represents a public place, a street scene, it would be a 'shallow' scene, ahead of the other scenes, probably in the first grooves on either side of the stage

torch: carried by a link-boy, hired to light the way through the streets. Wycherley keeps up the illusion that the action of the play is continuous through a single day: it is now late evening

presently: immediately

a great bubble by his similes: judging from the comparisons Sparkish has just made ('false as dice' and so on), he must have been deceived many times

married your portion: married you for your money

stale wench: a mistress one has tired of

Act Five Scene Four

Horner's lovemaking is interrupted by the arrival of Lady Fidget, Mrs Fidget and Mrs Squeamish, so he locks Margery inside and comes to see the ladies. They have brought bottles of liquor with them and soon start singing and drinking freely. They also talk freely, about men and sex, and thus reveal their true natures to Horner. Although literally masked, they are in another sense unmasked in this scene and their hypocrisy laid bare. They all confess that Horner has been their lover, although each had thought she was the only one. So long as they preserve their 'honour' or public reputation they don't care.

Sir Jasper Fidget and Old Lady Squeamish come in, only to be bundled into another room along with the three ladies, while Horner releases Margery and is about to send her home when the arrival of more visitors makes it necessary to shut her up again. The new visitors are Pinchwife, Sparkish and Alithea accompanied by Harcourt and Lucy. They have a parson with them. They have come to sort out the confusion over the letter and the charge that Alithea is Horner's lover. Horner, in order to save Margery, says it is true that Alithea is his lover, and Pinchwife insists that they should marry here and now. But Margery rushes out of hiding when she thinks Pinchwife is going to draw his sword on Horner and the whole situation now is thrown into confusion, for she is dressed in Alithea's clothes. The others, Sir Jasper Fidget and all the ladies, come in again and ask what the matter is. Sir Jasper tries to tell Pinchwife that Horner couldn't have seduced Margery because he is impotent. Lucy tries to clarify matters by confessing that she gave Margery the idea of disguising herself as Alithea. To protect Margery Lucy insists that Margery doesn't love Horner, but Margery interrupts to say this isn't true. Quack and Dorilant enter and, to protect Horner, insist that he is impotent. Margery tries to deny this, from personal experience, but she is drowned out by the chorus of assurance from the other ladies that it is true. Doubtfully, Pinchwife accepts that it must be so. The play ends with a dance, and Horner's secret is preserved.

NOTES AND GLOSSARY:

The Scene changes again to HORNER's lodging: this would be a matter of drawing back the two flats painted to represent Covent Garden for V.3. The scene for Horner's lodgings, used for V.2, would then stand revealed

A table, banquet and bottles: what is implied here is that as Horner comes through one of the stage doors, as if from his bedroom, he finds Lady Fidget and the others already seated around his table, on which are the bottles and light refreshments, sent in by Sir Jasper (see V.2.100)

brimmer: glass

red: make-up. The wine will flush their cheeks better than rouge could

a good shape: a good figure. The wine will make them fat

'twill come to the glasses anon: they'll be throwing the glasses over their heads soon

stuffs:	materials, clothes
druggets:	inferior cloth
expectation:	waiting
sharp bent:	very hungry
ordinary:	tavern or eating-house
Falling on briskly:	eating up quickly
receivers:	waiting-women (needing to be bribed)
pass your grants:	accept your favours
Harry Common:	Horner is shared by, or 'common' to, them all

Exit HORNER *at t'other door*: that is, one of the stage doors at the side of the stage. At this moment the stage is entirely clear, a rare thing in Restoration comedy, where all is usually hustle and bustle. Here it is the calm before the storm of the last section of the play

mainly:	heartily
a combination:	a plot

Peeping in behind: Margery has come out a little through the stage door at the side of the stage and the others have not seen her yet. She wouldn't be 'behind' them or she couldn't be seen by the audience. She does not 'enter' until ten lines later

with his hat over his eyes: in the theatre, a traditional sign of grief

communicated:	had intercourse
French capon:	castrated cock, hence a eunuch
cast:	throw (of dice)
edify:	improve
murrain:	cattle disease
ballet:	merry dance
keep a pother:	make a fuss

Epilogue

The actress who played Lady Fidget addresses the men in the audience, especially those who pretend to be tough, womanising types. She describes men who are all talk, chasing women and then backing away on one excuse or another, and men who boast of their conquests which nobody believes in. Such types, for all their fine air and fine clothes, do more wrong to women than to husbands. Perhaps they might learn from Horner that instead of boasting if they pretend to have *no* successes with women people might be more likely to believe them and take them for gallants. But they must still be careful: they might deceive the world this way, but they'll never deceive women.

NOTES AND GLOSSARY:

Mistress Knep: the actress who played Lady Fidget, well-known at the time. She was also a singer. As with the prologue, the epilogue is a means of bridging the world of the play and the world of social reality. The playwright takes a feminist point of view and tells the men in the audience that women will always know the truth about their sexual prowess

vizard-mask: facemask. Prostitutes often wore masks in the theatre, so 'vizard-mask' means prostitute

stout: brave

tiring-room: dressing room

Falstaffs: liars. Falstaff, in Shakespeare's *Henry IV Part I*, boasted that he killed robbers in buckram suits, and as he told the story the number of robbers grew from two to eleven

buckram maidenheads: imaginary virgins

essenced: perfumed

Flanders mares: powerful horses; here 'mistresses'

picquet, ombre, loo: various card-games popular at the time

coz'ning: fooling, deceiving

Part 3

Commentary

General

If you are coming to study Restoration comedy for the first time, *The Country Wife* may be something of a shock. Even if you are already familiar with a play or two from this period, such as Etherege's (?1634–92) *The Man of Mode* (1676) or William Congreve's *The Way of the World* (1700), you may still find *The Country Wife* something of a shock. It may seem more crude, more pornographic, than you expected. It is well, then, before entering into an analysis of the dramatic features of the play, to clarify somewhat the nature of this comedy and to clear the way for a serious consideration of its artistic merits.

The Country Wife is meant to be shocking. It would be foolish to turn aside its brutal aspects, its heartlessness and explicit treatment of human sexuality, as if these were not present at all. We must not think, either, that the author was unaware he was being crude and shocking. One sometimes meets the kind of criticism which takes this line: 'in a play like *The Country Wife* people are depicted as deceitful, hypocritical, shallow, mean-minded, and at the same time sex-crazy; the author doesn't seem to condemn these people, so why should we bother to give them our attention, since they are worthless creatures, beneath our serious notice.' This is to ignore the way *The Country Wife* hangs together as a play, unified in tone, style and form, so that it makes a statement about how people act in a certain society. When an author is in control of his material in this way, as will be shown in the commentary that follows, we are in the world of art not of pornography. Art is concerned with a criticism of life; pornography, even if it pretends to disapprove, is essentially concerned only to arouse sexual feelings in the reader. Art provides perception, insight; pornography provides a peep-show without any broadening of one's knowledge of humanity. Both can cause a shock to the reader, but the shock of art is to the mind as well as to the senses.

Another point to be made here is that *The Country Wife* is written in that age-old form, comedy. Now comedy from its very origins, in ancient Greece, had two functions which fed into the overall result, which was laughter. These functions were ridicule and celebration. On the one hand, ridicule or insult was thrown at whatever was regarded as repressive, that is all sources of restraint, disapproval or destruction.

There was a certain lee-way or licence granted to the writers of comedy, from ancient times on, whereby the mockery of decency or of law and order or of new trends or directions, was tolerated by society. The idea here probably was that it was a good thing for audiences occasionally to see attacks made on approved figures in society or on established laws, because this let off steam, or, we might say, it defused social tensions and (by laughter) reconciled people to the way things were in life. On the other hand, comedy enacted a celebration of fertility. It would appear that obscenity was always a part of the activity or rituals of comedy, so that bodily functions and in particular human reproduction were mimicked. People always laugh at such vulgarity, but the laughter releases fear and consolidates, as it were, the normal and natural functions whereby life is continued. As comedy became, with the passing of time, more sophisticated, this comic theme became embodied in a love story, so that plays invariably ended with the marriage of the young lovers. This marriage symbolised not only the continuity of society but also the kind of victory over death and repression which comedy had always celebrated. The marriage feast, usually signalled by a dance, celebrated this idea in a joyous image. Comedy thus has always endorsed sex, though usually within the bounds approved by society, namely marriage.

It will be seen below, when the play is explored in detail, that Wycherley's *The Country Wife* does not exactly conform to this rough-and-ready outline of the nature and functions of comedy. For one thing, as must be obvious to you if you have read the play at all (and if you have not, let me urge you here to put down this book and pick it up again only when you *have* read *The Country Wife*), that it treats marriage very boldly indeed. It seems to approve of sex outside marriage, especially in the case of Margery, the country wife herself. It doesn't punish the man who threatens what is usually referred to as the sanctity of marriage, namely Horner. And this is one major reason why we get the kind of criticism of *The Country Wife* already referred to above: as if the play were fundamentally immoral.

What you should consider, however, is that the playwright would be well aware himself of how he was presenting marriage here (and don't forget that there *is* a celebration of marriage in the play, that of Alithea to Harcourt, quite in the traditional style). Wycherley, we must believe, deliberately presented an attack on a certain kind of marriage: not on marriage itself. Therefore, we must not be too hasty in forming moral judgments about this play. It is more intelligent to begin with the assumption that it is a fairly complex structure, for which simple and obvious moral ideas (on our part) will not do. This complexity will be explored more fully in the commentary that follows, but for the moment it is worth bearing in mind these three points:

1. Being a comedy, *The Country Wife* is partly concerned with mocking some widely accepted ideas or practices. We must maintain an overall view if we are to keep a sane and balanced attitude towards the targets of Wycherley's mockery.

2. Again, being a comedy, *The Country Wife* is partly concerned with a celebration of life's continuity, its triumph over whatever threatens to repress natural spirits or to kill growth. Our attitude towards the treatment of sex in the play should be directed accordingly. We will soon find that, if we keep in mind the play as a whole, the seeming immorality is actually a challenge to the audience to examine their standards of judgment. The play, like any good work of art, has a way of revising our views for us.

3. Comedy is critical, that is, it makes a criticism of society; and it works best when the audience understands this and becomes critical in spirit also. In reading a play this usually means maintaining an open mind and letting the mind 'play' with the text. It is best to leave judgment or evaluation aside, until the play is over and can be fully considered.

Characters

Wycherley's method of characterisation is to allow characters, while presenting one face (the face they wish others to judge them by), to reveal another: the underlying, real face. All the time, we are required to discriminate between the two faces, one of which is no more than a mask. As Harcourt remarks in the play: 'Most men are the contraries to that they would seem' (1.1.251). Much of the comedy lies in the way the characters slip on and off this mask, because this habit or practice shows us the way society operates. In this manner, characters who are in one sense 'types', such as the jealous husband or the money-grubbing husband or the foolish rival, serve to show a whole, general way of life. Various types represent pieces of a philosophy of life, so that together they form a jig-saw picture of a world based on certain values. Wycherley's comedy builds up this world picture and allows us to see its shortcomings and absurdities.

In order to provide us with a picture of his society, revealed by its own representatives, Wycherley divided his characters into two groups. On the one hand there are those who are satirised in a fairly straightforward way, Pinchwife, Sparkish, Sir Jasper Fidget and the so-called 'virtuous gang', Lady Fidget, Dainty Fidget, Mrs Squeamish and Old Lady Squeamish. On the other hand, in contrast to this group, there are the characters with whom we are meant to sympathise in varying degrees, Margery Pinchwife, Alithea and Harcourt. The minor characters, Quack and Lucy, also belong here. Horner stands outside both groups, watching, smiling, manipulating, rather like the playwright himself. His is the most difficult role to assess, because he seems to belong to both groups: ambivalently, he is both despicable and admirable. We shall see how the complexity of Horner's relationship to the action renders the play rich and fascinating in its comic power.

We shall first examine the group of characters who, collectively, form the 'world of the play' that is satirised, and then move on to the other, sympathetic group, before tackling Horner and interpreting the play.

Pinchwife

On the one hand, Pinchwife is a man who is wronged by Horner, and he could be seen as a husband desperately trying to maintain his wife's virtue in the face of the depravity of city life. But on the other hand he is so mean, so suspicious and so nasty that his wife's eventual adultery is not at all surprising, and we tend to regard it as just punishment for his nastiness. In other words, we see in the characterisation here a model of what Wycherley does in a more complex way in the play as a whole: he modifies our perceptions of good and bad by providing us with a larger frame of reference than that supplied by the letter of the law. Let us see if we can make this more clear by analysing Pinchwife's character and role in the play.

Pinchwife locks up his pretty wife Margery not because he has a high regard for her virtue and wants to protect it but because he has a low regard for human nature and for women in particular. Women are not to be trusted; they are worse liars than men (II.1.330−1) and have 'more desires . . . more lust, and more of the devil' (IV.2.58−9). His constant refrain is 'I understand the town' (1.1.405−6, and frequently afterwards). He is a cynic, with the cynic's anxiety that his own base habits are practised by everyone. In his younger days, as Horner tells us (1.1.349−50), Pinchwife was himself a London libertine: he kept mistresses and was known as a 'whoremaster'.

He has not so much reformed in marrying Margery as retreated from the scene of corruption, as he sees it. Thus his 'dreadful apprehensions' (III.1.36) about London are based on his own experience and reflect his own knowledge. Also, his anxiety to keep Margery in ignorance of the ways of London men has nothing to do with caring for her, in a loving way. Rather it has to do with holding on to what he has got, as if Margery were a piece of property. He speaks of her as 'my own freehold' (II.1.301−2) and often equates her with money: 'He that shows his wife *or money* will be in danger of having them borrowed sometimes' (III.2.345−6 my italics; compare V.2.79−82). There is thus no love in the man: he is a miser who hoards Margery as he might any precious thing, solely for his own pleasure. As Horner tells him: 'you only married to keep a whore to yourself' (I.1.431). Pinchwife's marriage has, in fact, nothing to do with love, for he says himself: 'he's a fool that marries, but he's a greater that does not marry a fool' (I.1.396–7).

Pinchwife's attitude towards everyone in the play, not just towards Horner, is negative. He disapproves of his sister Alithea's natural way of seeing people and being seen in London, and tries to suggest she is immoral for talking to Margery about the attractions of London life. He blames her when Margery slips away, calling her 'thou legion of bawds . . . Damned, damned sister!' (III.2.512–15), hardly the language of a caring brother. The real proof of Pinchwife's degradation, however, lies in the fact that he is prepared to lead his own sister to Horner for his pleasure, as a means of keeping Horner away from his wife. This is the negation of all love, and it comes about through Pinchwife's own selfishness. He is negative also towards Sparkish, his opposite so far as his attitude towards women is concerned. Pinchwife regards him as a fool, and urges him repeatedly to deny Harcourt access to Alithea. When it suits him he takes Alithea away from Sparkish and gives her to Horner, without in the least considering the happiness of either party. He is similarly negative towards Sir Jasper Fidget and his wife's company: he will neither socialise with them nor allow them to see Margery.

Thus everything about Pinchwife is negative and against life's joy, life's fulness and life's expansion. He is the perfect target for the comic spirit to mock, tease, cheat and outwit. His jealousy is merely an aspect of his meanness; his habit of locking up Margery merely proof of his miserliness. The real Pinchwife comes out in moments of violence, when he draws a penknife or a sword on Margery and threatens to mutilate her beauty if she doesn't do what he wishes (IV.2 and IV.4). Here we see the savagery behind the protective husband, and it is quite logical that he should similarly draw his sword on Horner in the end (V.4.270, 286), for Horner is the catalyst of Pinchwife's self-revelation. Through Horner's 'positive' powers, which Pinchwife irrationally fears, Pinchwife is led to expose himself as a fool. It is vital to note, finally, that Pinchwife is the only one in the play who does not know that Horner is supposed to be impotent. It happens not to be true, of course, but Pinchwife's ignorance of the rumour shows how deaf he is to the world around him. He is anti-social, immersed totally in himself and his own possessions. He fully deserves to be cheated, because this informs the audience how necessary it is to be the opposite of cynical and selfish, if one is not to be absurdly inhuman.

Sparkish

The kindest thing that can be said about Sparkish is that he is a fool. When you first read the play you may well be inclined to dismiss him as utterly improbable, a character so naive and gullible as to be totally incredible. But if you read the play a second time, and look closely at Sparkish and his relationship with Alithea, you will notice that he is not simply an ass, a half-wit, but a pretender, one who thinks he is the epitome of fashion all the time. In that regard he is a type character, the fop or dandy, very popular on the Restoration stage from this time on.

As with Pinchwife, the characterisation of Sparkish follows a two-pronged or dualistic method. Sparkish assumes himself to be a broad-minded, tolerant man, for whom jealousy is out of the question. Jealousy would be a sign of unsophistication, to his mind, and he thinks of himself as so sophisticated and elegant that he couldn't ever stoop to suspicion either of his fiancée or of his male friends. But when it is shown to him (as he thinks) by Pinchwife that Alithea betrayed him and jilted him for Horner, he suddenly displays a cruelty and a bitterness towards Alithea which were well hidden before. So the real Sparkish emerges under pressure, and it is a reality which shows how mistaken Alithea was in her regard for his feelings. She gets a lesson in moral discrimination, which we also share. As a rival to Harcourt he dwindles in stature until his true worthlessness is entirely apparent, and his mask of social poise and generosity is ripped off to reveal the insignificant figure beneath.

It is no great problem to find the evidence for this in the text of *The Country Wife*. Perhaps it would be worthwhile for the student if you attempted to do some of this for yourself. Here are some of the headings under which to look in the text for appropriate references:

Sparkish as a would-be wit: When he meets Horner, Dorilant and Harcourt he tries to impress them with references to social engagements, aristocratic acquaintances and skill at clever talk.

Sparkish's attitude towards Alithea is that she may, indeed, be a beautiful woman, but that he, being a busy man-about-town, must not be expected to spend too much time seeing her or talking to her. He reveals in Act Five that he was interested mainly in her money. He insults her in an unforgiveable way at this point.

Sparkish's attitude towards Harcourt is that Harcourt's admiration for Alithea provides social approval of Sparkish's own taste. He is not jealous, because he is too stupid to see that Harcourt is genuinely attracted to Alithea and makes love to her before Sparkish's eyes.

Sparkish's attitude towards Pinchwife, his prospective brother-in-law, is that of the easy, tolerant lover towards the unnecessarily jealous man. Sparkish's claim, to be 'frank' and 'free' is eventually thrown back at him when Pinchwife shows him the result of his tolerance, namely, the supposed infidelity of Alithea.

Sparkish as man-about-town: he makes many references to the king and his court at Whitehall, and to the theatre where he goes as a matter of course when there's a new play on. He goes to such places only to be seen. His view of playwrights is actually hostile, as he is afraid they will depict him in a play. Thus he merely *pretends* to be a cultured man.

Wycherley's success in portraying this dandy led to a new trend in the theatre. The following year, in 1676, Sir George Etherege had an outstanding hit with *The Man of Mode; or, Sir Fopling Flutter*, in which the last-named character, an imitator of all the latest French fashions and a blockhead who tries to be a clever fellow, was enormously popular with the London audience. The fop thereafter became the essential comic character in Restoration plays. Wycherley paved the way for this trend with his depiction of the superficial, dandified Sparkish.

Sir Jasper Fidget

Sir Jasper is one of those cuckolded by Horner in the play. He is meant, one presumes, to stand for many. His only purpose is to make *use* of Horner. His visit to Horner in the first scene, when he brings Lady Fidget and her sister with him, suggests that Sir Jasper is heartless and opportunistic. After all, so far as he knows, Horner is a man suffering from a disease which has left him entirely impotent; and yet Sir Jasper finds this hilariously funny and a reason for teasing Horner: 'Ha, ha, ha! I'll plague him yet' (1.1.71). He wants not only to taunt Horner, and thereby assert his own superiority over him, but also to off-load on to him his social responsibilities as a husband. It is he and not Horner who takes the initiative here. This is the whole point behind Wycherley's satire. Sir Jasper, self-interested to the point of greed, can hardly wait to exploit the sufferings of another fellow human being so as to provide himself with more leisure for business: after he has successfully begged Horner, in Act Two, to act as escort to his wife and the other ladies, he says: 'Therefore, now you like him, get you gone to your business together; go, go, to your business, I say, pleasure, whilst I go to my pleasure, business' (II.1.563–6).

Therefore, as in all comedies where greed is being exposed – Ben Jonson's (1572–1637) *Volpone* (1605) being an outstanding example here also – it is plain that the greedy man will do anything to gain his ends, and that the so-called villain (Horner, in this case) has only to remain passive. The greedy man will take the initiative himself, and that is precisely what makes him comic, for he digs, as it were, his own comic grave. Thus Sir Jasper, in anticipation of the action of Pinchwife in Act Five, brings his own wife to Horner and presses her on him, and gives him 'all sorts of freedom' with her (II.1.508). He stands revealed, then, not just as foolish but as a man sexually inadequate himself and in search of a substitute who would at once relieve him of his responsibility and yet be harmless. His intended cruelty marks him off as rather similar to Pinchwife. Consequently he gets what he deserves and it is fitting that *he never finds out the truth.*

Lady Fidget and the 'virtuous gang'

In depicting Lady Fidget and the 'virtuous gang', as they call themselves (V.2.94), Wycherley's comic skill is seen at its best. These ladies go about with an air of moral decency. They are so delicate in their sensibilities that they cannot bear even to *hear* the word 'naked' (II.1.396), much less countenance any kind of immorality. But the first time they are alone (as at II.1.332–87) they reveal another side of their natures, totally opposite to the modest and pure side presented in public. Privately, their conversation is full of references to affairs, sexual pleasure and how best to preserve their good names. Thus the central fact about these women is that they wear a social mask, behind which appetite rages.

Horner knows the hypocrisy of these women from the outset. Indeed he says so straight to Lady Fidget's face in the first scene: 'your virtue is your greatest affectation, madam' (I.1.94). His ability to seduce all three of them, while still they maintain their demure public attitude of propriety, proves his point. All that matters, so far as Lady Fidget is concerned, is that her 'honour', by which she means simply her good name, should be preserved. The same holds true for Mrs Dainty Fidget and Mrs Squeamish, and the joke is trebled when Horner privately tells the truth to the others also and subsequently enjoys their favours.

The scenes that most graphically reveal the comic contradictions underlying the behaviour of the 'virtuous gang', are, firstly, the 'china' scene and, secondly, the 'drinking' scene. It is appropriate to look at each of these briefly.

The 'china' scene: this is the scene of the assignation between Horner and Lady Fidget (IV.3). In her usual coy manner, she tells Horner when she comes in: 'But first, my dear sir, you must promise to have a care of my dear honour' (IV.3.41–2). When he tries to make her act naturally by asking her to drop all this talk of her 'honour', she insists that one cannot be too careful: 'oh 'tis a wicked censorious world, Mr Horner!' (line 60). It is clear from this that she really is terrified of what people might say, they 'are so censorious and detracting' (lines 60–1). But it is entirely dishonest of her to pretend she is virtuous only for fear of what people might say. For she is a woman of strong sexual passions, which she hides beneath a veneer of staid respectability. Just how strong those passions are is made clear when her husband breaks in on this romantic assignation. Far from giving up the rendezvous, Lady Fidget seems to become more excited by the danger implied by her husband's presence, and runs off inside to Horner's bedroom, fully intending that Horner shall follow, as indeed he does. When eventually she comes out, to an ever-increasing audience on stage, she indicates by her double-meaning language how fiercely she has been making love. She pretends she has been persuading Horner to give her a piece of china. What is comic here, undoubtedly, is the incongruity between her manner of outward respectability (collecting china was a fashionable pastime) and the truth regarding her sexual nature. Horner has allowed us to see into the nature of a fashionable married woman of the day. In quick succession, we see likewise into the appetites of Mrs Dainty Fidget and Mrs Squeamish, who are similarly eager to share Horner's bed. Collectively, then, these three women reveal how false the image is of womankind that society fosters and sets up as a standard.

The 'drinking' scene: in a way, this scene is a continuation of the 'china' scene, because here the implications of that scene are made crystal clear. Indeed, you may wonder if Wycherley doesn't overdo it here, by underlining what scarcely needs much further exemplification. But perhaps the real value of the scene lies in the fact that here the 'virtuous gang' think they are in private, and completely safe, and so they let their masks (literally) come off, speaking more frankly than at any other time in the play. This they would never do in a man's presence were it not that each one believes that Horner has had only her; each thinks she is his secret lover; and because of his presumed impotence he will not betray their confidence. The effect of Horner's presence, while they drink freely and talk even more freely about their attitudes towards men, is like a truth serum. For his part, Horner steers the conversation round to the topics he wants them to discuss and to confess about, so that they implicate themselves irredeemably in dishonesty. It is as if he had a tape-recorder hidden in the room, gathering the evidence that would damn these women forever. In that sense, the scene is a trial scene, and the audience is allowed access to the tapes that damn the behaviour of a certain set of women beyond all reasonable doubt.

Horner first gets the women to confess that they use their 'reputations' as forbidding, chaste beings 'only to deceive the world with less suspicion' (V.4.100). Or, as Lady Fidget goes on to say, with the shocking frankness of one who does not expect to be quoted: 'Our virtue is like the statesman's religion, the Quaker's word, the gamester's oath, and the great man's honour – but to cheat those that trust us.' This last phrase couldn't but cause a gasp to run through Wycherley's first audience. It is a shocking attack on the simpering modesty of those who use an appearance of virtue only 'to cheat those that trust us'. But why, Horner asks, do these women pretend so much to possess this virtue, this 'honour'? And the answer comes back quite frankly: 'to enjoy the better and more privately those you love' (lines 115–16). It's all a game, all a means towards increasing the thrill of extra-marital sex. Honour, Horner concludes, and none of the ladies contradicts him, is meaningless. It has no objective value, but depends altogether on what individuals believe it to be (lines 167–8). Like a jewel, Lady Fidget says, it shines just as brightly even if it is 'counterfeit' (line 165). The 'virtuous gang' are thus clearly shown and seen to be anything but virtuous, and the effect is, finally, to mock the abuse and denial of natural appetite in deference to an empty code of good behaviour.

Turning now to the other main group, those treated sympathetically in the play, let us begin with the country wife herself.

Margery Pinchwife

It has to be understood that at this time the epithet 'country' signified 'ignorant' and 'ridiculous' in the minds of London people, especially those who aspired to 'good taste'. The town was regarded as the centre of civilisation, intellectual life and (royally supervised) order. The country was looked on as disorder: rough, unmannerly, hostile to all comfort and elegance of mind and body. A country wife, accordingly, would be regarded as somewhat uncouth, as Margery Pinchwife is to a distinct degree. She is thus, in part, ridiculous. She has no idea how to behave or how to talk in polite society. Her naïveté, her sheer innocence, blinds her to the dangers inherent in meeting and going off with the likes of Horner. She does not know, as Alithea discovers, that a lady must not go 'a-walking' alone in London (II.1.24). She speaks in a kind of baby-talk when addressing Pinchwife, even in public, and entirely lacks the polish of someone like Alithea.

Yet, in spite of her awkwardness, Margery is presented as lovable and refreshing. This is largely because she is young and beautiful as well as raw and ignorant. Horner falls for her when he first sees her in the theatre: 'She was exceedingly pretty', he tells Pinchwife, 'I was in love with her at that distance' (1.1.448–9). When he meets her close up for the first time, in III.2, even though she is disguised as a boy, Horner doubts if ever he saw a lovelier creature. That, of course, is why Pinchwife keeps her locked up, or only lets her out under certain circumstances. Her natural beauty, then, makes Margery's awkwardness charming. (Remember that the role was always played by a pretty actress, *not* a boy dressed up.) Moreover, even if she is raw and unsophisticated, she is neither backward nor boisterous (what came to be known as 'Hoydenish' in such types) but lively in a most engaging way. She learns quickly how to write a love letter, in spite of Pinchwife's desire to the contrary (IV.2). In a masterly scene later on (V.1) she shows how quick-witted she can be, when she dresses up as Alithea and very nimbly fools Pinchwife into believing he has locked her up while she has in fact skipped round to his other side as Alithea.

She is genuinely attracted to Horner, and (in contrast to the 'virtuous gang') is prepared to risk everything – her good name and even her life – to save him from either injury or insult (V.4). It may well be felt that she is much too good for Horner, but the point to bear in mind is that her innocence introduces a breath of fresh air into this society, with its hot-house atmosphere of good manners and hidden hypocrisies. Her open admission of desire is beautifully expressed in her letter to Horner: 'I'm sure if you and I were in the country at cards together . . . I could not help treading on your toe under the table . . . or rubbing knees with you, and staring in your face 'till you saw me . . . and then looking down and blushing for an hour together' (IV.2.155−60). The picture is innocent; it is also honest and vivid. Margery stands in the play as the embodiment of natural impulses, which, alas, experience in the town must eventually turn into sophisticated dishonesty. At the end she is persuaded to shut up when her impulse is to burst out with the truth about Horner's impotence to clear his name: 'for to my certain knowledge . . . ' (V.4.360−1).

Through this character Wycherley is saying that because of the nature of London life and London manners, innocence (which Pinchwife mistakes for ignorance) inevitably comes to 'certain knowledge', and with that experience honesty in relationships inevitably ceases. Thus while he celebrates the sexual impulse by means of the joyous beauty of Margery's character, Wycherley cannot (because he is writing realism) allow it the traditional outlet of a happy marriage. The nature of the society which Wycherley is mocking and criticising makes it necessary for Margery to adjust her impulses to the ethos of the town. She must learn to be deceitful, and to repress nature under a guise of seeming. We find this shocking; but it is the nature of society itself we ought to find shocking.

Alithea and Harcourt

It often happens in comedy that the lovers are the least interesting figures. It is usually the rival lover or lovers, or the clever servant (or clown), or the forbidding father or mother figure, who attracts most attention and gives most entertainment. Yet, for its meaning, the play as a whole centres on the lovers. Since it is an imitation of the very life-process itself, the triumph of vitality over deadliness, the comedy treats seriously the love affair which ends in a marriage anticipated and approved by the audience. Such is the case with Alithea and Harcourt.

There is nothing remarkable about either character. Both are reasonably intelligent, quick to discern the failings of those around them, whether the foolishness of Pinchwife's jealousy (in Alithea's case) or the unworthiness of Sparkish's affections (in Harcourt's case). Both characters, however, hold themselves aloof from the hypocrisy and double-dealing of London life. Neither wears a mask (of respectability or good opinion), because both believe still in the possibility of plain dealing; but Harcourt has to make use of disguise and deceit in order to outwit Sparkish and marry Alithea. This stratagem, however, is forced upon Harcourt because of the reluctance of Alithea to abandon Sparkish. We approve of Harcourt's deceit here because it has a life-giving purpose: it is not the kind of deceit which is hypocritical. It is a practical means of achieving a proper marriage.

A significant feature of the relationship of Harcourt and Alithea is the play of wit between them. Harcourt is a typical Restoration hero, clever, handsome and fond of women. He has, in fact, had many lovers, a matter he regards as healthy and normal: 'mistresses are like books – if you pore upon them too much they doze you [make you drowsy] and make you unfit for company, but if used discreetly you are the fitter for conversation by 'em' (1.1.198–200). Like most Restoration heroes, he thinks little of marriage. Marriage was regarded as a trap; pursuit of women outside of marriage was the young man's occupation. But, conventionally, when such a young man or libertine met the right girl he was transformed, and would suffer *even* marriage in order to win this beauty. So it is with Harcourt. When he meets Alithea (in II.1) it is a case of love at first sight. They are introduced by Sparkish, who describes Harcourt as 'a man of such perfect honour, he would say nothing to a lady he does not mean' (II.1.146–7). This happens to be true, so that Harcourt immediately tells Sparkish he envies him: 'till nów I never thought I should have envied you *or any man about to marry*, but you have the best excuse for marriage I ever knew' (lines 154–6, my italics). Alithea, displaying her ready wit, assumes that Harcourt is simply teasing Sparkish here, 'since you are an enemy to marriage' (lines 159–60). There follows a rapid exchange between them, typical of the witty repartee to be expected between lovers in Restoration comedy; indeed this is one way of knowing they are meant for each other. For example:

HARCOURT: Truly, madam, I never was an enemy of marriage till now, because marriage was never an enemy to me before.
ALITHEA: But why, sir, is marriage an enemy to you now? Because

it robs you of your friend here? For you look upon a friend married as one gone into a monastery, that is dead to the world.

(II.1.162–7)

In the scene that follows, this readiness of wit is plainly seen. The point of difference between them is Sparkish, whom Harcourt wants her to abandon but whom she feels obliged to retain as her fiancé. Even when Alithea tries to tell Sparkish that Harcourt is making love to her the play of wit continues, as Harcourt does not stop but cleverly woos her by criticising Sparkish to her face. Later, in IV.1, Harcourt's wit takes a practical form when he disguises himself as a clergyman and prevents the marriage of Sparkish to Alithea.

The verbal fencing that goes on between Harcourt and Alithea, then, identifies them as perfectly suited to each other. But blocking any further progress is Alithea's stubborn fidelity to Sparkish. She feels morally bound to marry him since she's promised to him. This is an admirable stance, but Alithea holds to it too rigidly. Even when Harcourt shows her beyond all doubt that Sparkish is a fool, and a vain one at that (III.2), she insists that as a matter of 'honour' (III.2.496) she must marry Sparkish. Here Wycherley obviously wants us to contrast this notion of 'honour' with that of Lady Fidget. Where Lady Fidget thinks of honour only as her good name, which she can preserve by keeping her misdemeanours private, Alithea thinks of honour as a moral obligation, something to be observed whether in public or private simply because it is right to do so. Can one go too far with such an ethic? Is Alithea being foolish in persisting with her promise to Sparkish? How is this question judged in the play?

Lucy, Alithea's maidservant, offers an opinion which may be instructive for an interpretation of this moral problem. On the morning of Alithea's marriage to Sparkish, Lucy tries to dissuade her from what she regards as a deadly union. Even though she admits to loving Harcourt and not loving Sparkish, Alithea insists that her sense of 'justice' will not allow her 'to deceive or injure' him (IV.1.17). Lucy points out that to marry without love is to do a greater injustice, and she then roundly condemns the whole concept of honour: 'But what a devil is this honour? 'Tis sure a disease in the head, like the megrim [migraine], or falling sickness, that always hurries people away to do themselves mischief. Men lose their lives by it; women what's dearer to 'em, their love, the life of life' (IV.1.28–32). So far as comedy is concerned, Lucy must be regarded as right. Alithea is too obsessed with an *idea* of honour, and she adheres to the principle mechanically. Usually when a character becomes mechanical, comedy makes it its business to criticise or poke fun. Alithea isn't made fun of, but she is made to suffer, to some degree, when she is accused in Act Five of being Horner's lover. With a vengeance, her honour is certainly thrown in question then, and there is nothing abstract or metaphysical about it. But it is at this point she sees for the first time what Sparkish is really like. He not only believes the slander, but turns extremely nasty about it saying: 'I never had any passion for you till now, for now I hate you' (V.3.66–7). Harcourt, on the other hand, when told about the slander, recognises it immediately as a lie: 'I will not only believe your innocence myself, but make all the world believe it' (V.4.250–2). He is determined to protect Alithea's 'honour', he tells Horner (lines 252–5). Since this is not a play in which duels are fought it is not necessary for Harcourt to act the true knight and risk his life for Alithea's honour. Yet his commitment to that cause is clear enough.

Horner

It is difficult to be sure about Horner. Is there more to him than his obscene names implies? Is he the Restoration rake magnified like a great cartoon? To some extent he *is* the Restoration hero who thinks of little else besides sex and conquest. He can't, it would seem, get enough of it. This is why he concocts this plan to proclaim himself impotent as a result of a stay in Paris, where he says he contracted syphilis, is now cured but incapable of having sex. His motive as he tells his friend Quack (1.1.), is simply to get more women into his bed.

But he has another, accompanying motive, and the problem is how to reconcile this with the first motive. The second motive is to prove, to his own satisfaction and that of his friend Quack, how one may still gain women in inverse proportion to one's attractiveness. He shows that what should repel women actually brings them flocking, because they find him 'safe'; he has a passport to their private rooms because of his known affliction. The question this raises in our minds is this: can Horner really *like* women, if all he wants to do is to show how hypocritical they can be? Or, looked at another way, does his cynicism on this subject make it impossible for us to have any sympathy for his whole plan? (*At this point, see if you can answer this question.*)

In fact, it is probably best to regard Horner as amoral, that is, as not being concerned at all, one way or the other, with morality. He is scientific in his approach to society, determining to apply a theory and prove its validity. He is, of course, also a Restoration type, a cynic, a wit, a despiser of marriage, and, as he puts it, 'a Machiavel in love' (IV.3. 66–7), a schemer and double-dealer. But above all he is intellectual in his attitude to life, even though he is a pleasure-seeker, a sensualist. Thus, for example, his wit is of the sort that searches for generalisations, revealing a mind which is analytic: 'women are as apt to tell before the intrigue as men after it, and so show themselves the vainer sex' (III.2.78–9). This is the remark of a man who has thought out his

ideas, based on close observation. His comments tend towards state-
ments which sum up general laws of behaviour (other examples of this
can be found at I.1.204–11; I.1.413–18; II.1.499–502; V.4.78–81
and 173–5). And we should recall his remark to Lady Fidget, when he
has told her he is not impotent: 'I desire to be tried only, madam'
(II.1.530). That is to say: 'make the experiment'. Horner is a comic
empiricist.

Horner is also a loner, even though he has his circle of friends. He
does *not* share his secret with these friends, and is not close to them
emotionally. He is far closer to Quack, who as a doctor shares in
Horner's scientific experiment. It is only with Quack that Horner con-
fers, and discusses the progress of his plan (as in IV.3). His solitude, his
tendency to preserve his secret for the sake of the experiment, underlines his scientific nature.

If, however, Horner is scientific, he is also cold. Among his friends,
to be sure, he is jolly and high-spirited, and among the ladies he is
always witty and attentive. But it is all calculating, all very carefully
controlled. We are shocked, in the end, to find that he is prepared to
tell a lie about Alithea, in order to protect Margery. His comment is: 'I
am still [always] on the criminal's side, against the innocent'
(V.4.223–4). We can't help but find this attitude appallingly lacking in
decency. Therefore, although we can understand that Horner is suc-
cessful in *demonstrating* how hypocritical women can be, we cannot
easily accept his self-interest or his indifference to Alithea's good
name. This is the crucial part of the play so far as our judgment of
Horner goes. It is impossible for us to avoid moral categories here, as
Horner himself does. We do *not* have to follow suit. If we keep our distance we can say: 'Yes, I see that this lively, clever fellow has exposed
the corruption of society, and that he is calculating enough not to get
emotionally entangled while doing so, but there is more to experience
than proving a hypothesis.' Horner is, essentially, an anti-social figure
– which is why he is against marriage – and as such he loses our sympathy before the end of the play.

Themes

It is well to bear in mind that *The Country Wife* was meant to be realistic. It was meant to be a mirror of the manners and character-types in
London in the year 1675. In the play itself Dorilant defends the playwrights of the day for the way they depict human nature: 'Blame 'em
not, they must follow their copy – the age' (III.2.120). Therefore, repeatedly throughout *The Country Wife* there is an emphasis on the
values by which the characters live. One could single out, as the most
significant values so dealt with: nature, honour and love.

Nature

By nature is meant here, human nature. Nature in the broader sense, meaning the world of experience or the powers that flow from the elements and govern human emotions, has no part in Restoration comedy. The focus is always narrow. We are concerned with human behaviour in a social context. But Wycherley is interested in probing and revealing human nature in this context, under the pressures of what is regarded as 'proper' in London life.

Horner and Margery are presented as two opposite versions of what being 'natural' means. Each has a hunger for experience, but Horner solves it negatively, Margery positively. They eventually come together, and the 'minus' and 'plus' properties interact so as to redefine the meaning of 'natural'.

To explain further. Horner is associated with (sexual) appetite, Margery with innocence. But Horner, in pretending to be impotent, is regarded as 'innocent' by Sir Jasper Fidget (1.1.112). So we have false innocence set against the real innocence of Margery. Her husband, Pinchwife, values this quality in her only because it implies ignorance of the way of the world: 'since silly and innocent', as he puts it, 'will not know the difference betwixt a man of one-and-twenty and one of forty' (1.1.388−90). Pinchwife's notion of nature, in this case, is protected inexperience. He wants to keep Margery in her natural ignorance of the ways of London life. His notion is that women would be much more manageable if left in their 'natural' ignorant state, but love destroys this simple arrangement: 'Love! 'Twas he gave women first their craft, their art of deluding. Out of nature's hands they came plain, open, silly, *and fit for slaves*, as she [nature] and heaven intended 'em, but damned love . . . ' (IV.2.50−3, my italics). The natural state of women, as Pinchwife sees it, is slavish, and he wants it to be so. But Margery learns, despite his prohibitions, that a larger world of experience exists outside his tyrannical control and she acquires the skills to share in it. She moves, then, from a state of nature to a state of experience, along a track which exposes the foolishness and limitations of the Pinchwife point of view. It is fitting that Horner should be the centre of her broadening experience: through him, raw nature is turned into knowledge. When Alithea tells Pinchwife at the end that 'your wife is yet innocent' (V.4.372) she is using the word 'innocent' in a different sense from that which Pinchwife wants it to mean, that is, 'ignorant'. Margery is no longer ignorant of the sexual goings-on of London society and how to be part of them; but she is 'innocent' in the eyes of Alithea and we must ask how this can be.

The answer would seem to be as follows: nature in this play is divided into two states – appetite and innocence. Appetite leads to experience, innocence leads on to knowledge. When appetite and innocence combine, when Horner and Margery meet and make love, a new condition arises. Margery learns that to survive in this society she must be two-faced, she must have a mask to present to the public world which hides the true or private feelings. *To be 'natural' in this sophisticated society is* to be skilful at the use of the mask; *to be able to deceive with style.* This protects others as well as yourself. In gratitude for this protection, society will agree to protect in turn. Thus when she shut up about Horner's secret Margery is called 'innocent'. She has entered the world of Lady Fidget and the others, who are 'innocent' only in that they are never caught out by their husbands. To be innocent in this world, then, is to be free from scandal. We must remember Horner's remark: 'I am still on the criminal's side, *against the innocent'* (V.4.223–4, my italics). When he says that, he is referring to Margery as 'the criminal': a huge turn-about in the play. Handling the theme in this way, Wycherley comments on the society of his day when to be urbane was, necessarily, to lose innocence.

Honour

We have seen above, in the commentary on the character of Alithea, that (as with 'nature') there are two notions of honour in this play. On the one hand there is Lady Fidget's notion, whereby honour equals reputation. This, in turn, corresponds to appearance. It is a notion of honour that is altogether concerned with what people might say; it is *not* based on principles of good and evil. On the other hand, there is Alithea's notion of honour – as explained in detail already – according to which honour is a moral idea, something that commands Alithea to refuse Harcourt's love simply because she is promised to Sparkish. This notion corresponds to, or at least is directed towards upholding, reality. It is not concerned with what people might say; it is concerned with principle, with being true to an idea of good and evil. Appearance and reality are at odds in the play (as they often are in comedy), for it is through confusions over which is which that the plot advances. But the meaning of the play, in its deeper sense than Horner's trick alone suggets, is bound up with the way appearance *versus* reality redefines the concept of honour. It is shown that Alithea's fairly rigid notion of honour won't do: Sparkish is simply unworthy of the sort of sacrifice and constancy Alithea was dedicating to him. On the other hand, Lady Fidget's notion of honour is clearly, and repeatedly, exposed as hypocrisy; so, it won't do either. What emerges is a synthesis, a concept of honour which is at once moral and pragmatic, or, in other words, a strong suggestion that honour in the strict sense (Alithea's sense) is impossible in this shallow society but that more flexibility is required. It is honourable not to let Margery reveal to Pinchwife the full truth about Horner, because Pinchwife deserves to be cheated. It is honourable not to en-lighten Sir Jasper Fidget about his wife and the 'virtuous gang' because this also would achieve little beyond shocking Sir Jasper, in all probab-ility, into an untimely grave. Honour is thus not a very high-minded notion in this society, secular and pleasure-seeking as it is. Wycherley is a realist; he holds that honour in society is a matter of live and let live.

Love

There are two views of love presented in the play. One is of love as a convenience, as a casual matter in which selfish ends are served. This sort of love is what Lady Fidget and the 'virtuous gang' believe in. It is not, in the strict sense, love at all but indulgence in sexual encounter. It can be called a 'convenience' because that is what it is to these people, and to Horner also: he 'serves' them and they him, under the bond of secrecy, and there is no more to it. The piece of china with which Lady Fidget emerges from Horner's bedroom (IV.3.180) signifies the material nature of this love: it is a commodity, a collector's item, a thing rather than an intangible experience between people. It may be said that so far as Sir Jasper is concerned this kind of love is a conven-ience also. Although he is, of course, unaware that Horner is actually having sex with his wife he is quite prepared to hand her over to him as companion, since this leaves Sir Jasper free to do what he wants, namely attend to his business (II.1.565–6).

There is, however, another kind of love in the play, based on a true regard for the other person. Where love as convenience is self-directed, love as a true relationship is directed toward someone else. Here the terms are the opposite of materialistic. Here love is not a thing, not a possession, nor even a matter of money. This is (in part) why Sparkish is ineligible: for him the loved one is a beautiful object to be shown off among his friends, like a new prize possession, reflecting credit on him-self; and in the end he confesses that he was also attracted to Alithea for her money (V.3.67–9), meaning the five thousand pounds, a huge sum in those days, mentioned earlier by Pinchwife (I.1.341–2). True love is a spiritual matter, such as Harcourt describes when he indirectly woos Alithea in the presence of Sparkish. When Sparkish asks him 'But how do you love her?' Harcourt answers: 'With all my soul' (III.2.290–1), and 'With the best and truest love in the world' (line 294). He also refers to her 'heavenly form' (line 314). A little later, Harcourt almost betrays himself when disguised as a clergyman, by saying he will go ahead, 'With all my soul, divine, heavenly creature, when you please' (IV.1.125–6). Sparkish thinks this sort of language quite appropriate to a clergyman, but it merely reveals (comically) his failure to appreciate true love. Harcourt is, in fact, the measure in the play of this true love, and it is significant that he says Alithea should take the man 'Who should in all justice be yours, he that loves you most', and he '*Claps his hand on his breast*' to indicate he means himself (III.2.302). This is significant because it links love and justice. And this is how the theme of love is worked out in *The Country Wife*. The two kinds of love achieve different kinds of justice. Sparkish is pushed aside, Harcourt and Alithea, as we would wish, are united. Margery and Horner are not exposed, nor are the 'virtuous gang', which shows that Wycherley's idea of comic justice was not the usual moral one found in Shakespeare (for example, in *The Merchant of Venice* or in *Twelfth Night*). As with 'nature' and 'honour', 'love' too is seen as having a higher and a lower form, but Wycherley tolerantly allows both to co-exist right to the end of the play. This means that his vision of life is easy-going, for he compromises between the higher and lower values in society.

An interpretation of the play

From all that has been said above, about the characters and the themes, the following summary can be made.

1. *The Country Wife* is a realistic comedy of manners, which holds the mirror up to London life in the reign of King Charles II.

2. The play is a satire as well as a comedy. Whereas it celebrates love and insists that 'the life of life' (in Lucy's phrase, IV.1.32) should triumph over all meanness and jealousy, it also attacks hypocrisy and stupidity.

3. The structure of the play is dialectical, that is, themes are handled by introducing two opposing versions which are then, in the course of the action, fused into a new version, a synthesis. This gives the play an analytic, almost scientific style, as if the playwright were in a laboratory, examining the social life of his day in accordance with clearly held (but not lofty) ideas of behaviour and morality.

4. The governing character, Horner, the one whose plan sets in motion the whole comic structure of the play, is himself imbued with the scientific spirit. This is quite in line with the intellectual tendency of the time, because the Royal Society, patronised by King Charles II, had been set up just after 1660 to establish new scientific methods and to encourage experiments. Unlike the situation today, the study of science was not then separated from the pursuit of the arts, and so writers such as John Dryden were not only poets and playwrights but members also of the Royal Society, and interested in the findings of science. Since

Wycherley had a position at the heart of the literary and intellectual life of his day, as playwright and as a member of the court of Charles, he would obviously have shared the contemporary interest in science and in investigation. *The Country Wife* reflects this interest. Apart from the character of Horner, the scientific spirit is also suggested by the use throughout the play of a plain prose style, the language of stage realism.

We do not look in *The Country Wife* for a moving love story, primarily. Neither do we look for boisterous comedy, knockabout farce or rollicking entertainment. It is a 'new' comedy inasmuch as it is realistic, sophisticated and occupied with the situations and predicaments of people from the middle and upper classes of English life. It is a restrained comedy of manners of the sort that provokes 'thoughtful laughter'. We could easily dismiss the play, as some have done, as either too obscene or too trivial to be of any significance. But to do so would be to fail to respond to a text that is deliberately provoking – as becomes clear to anyone who takes the trouble to read Wycherley's next play, *The Plain Dealer* (1676). There he is much more angry at the ways of the world, that is, of fashionable London society, than he appears to be in *The Country Wife*. He may in fact have written this play before *The Country Wife*, but if so he inserted one scene later. In a passage in *The Plain Dealer* (II.1.) he has a discussion of the 'china' scene from which it is obvious that he meant it to be not merely erotic or obscene but to be taken intelligently as a comment on how people use language. Wycherley became known as 'Manly' Wycherley after this, after the hero, the 'plain dealer' or outspoken hero of that play. He was the kind of author who called a spade a spade and so he used comedy to reveal the games people play, the self-deceptions and subterfuges they engage in, in the name of competitive, urban living. He shows the seamy side of life, but he does this honestly and as a cause for laughter. When we laugh at what we see in *The Country Wife* it is because we are learning something about human nature that strikes us as both truthful and absurd.

It has to be said, however, that although *The Country Wife* was popular on the London stage until the middle of the eighteenth century, it fell into disrepute after that time and disappeared from the stage until the 1920s. It was because of the play's daring, or as some would say its immorality, that it thus faded from prominence. Public taste in England began to alter as early as the 1690s, and by the 1700s there were many attacks on drama and the theatres because of their so-called immorality and profanity. It was felt that drama should teach a clear lesson, and therefore comedies began to be written of an altogether different kind from *The Country Wife*. These new comedies, known as 'sentimental' comedies, offered characters of refinement and delicacy, whose manners and morals could be taken as models by the new middle-class audiences. Wycherley fell out of fashion. But the strongest attack came from the Victorians. Lord Macaulay, in particular, presented the view that *The Country Wife* was unfit for decent people to read (it was not likely to be seen on stage): 'We will not go into details. In truth, Wycherley's indecency is protected against the critics as a skunk is protected against the hunters. It is safe, because it is too filthy to handle, and too noisome [evil-smelling] even to approach.'* The Victorian attitude lasted until modern times. But once *The Country Wife* was revived on stage, in 1924, its theatrical virtues began to overshadow its so-called literary vices. It began to be staged at intervals up to 1956, when the English Stage Company gave a significant production at the Royal Court Theatre, London. After that date, *The Country Wife* found its place in the repertory of English masterpieces of comedy, and has even been seen on television. It would seem that modern audiences, unlike the Victorians, have no problems with the theme. Perhaps we live in a more frank and outspoken age – or possibly a more honest age? At any rate, it is worth bearing in mind that for a long time this play was too 'hot' for theatres to handle.

* *Critical and Historical Essays*, Longmans, London, 1870, p.585.

Part 4

Hints for study

Assessing the comic action

It sometimes happens that students spend too much time on character-isation, when assessing a comedy, and not enough on the comic action. The commentary in Part 3 tried to combine both, by discussing characters and themes together, and by placing these in the context of the play as a whole. But it is well to spend a little time here on 'the play as a whole' and how to seize hold of it critically.

When reading a comedy you should keep the motives of the characters clearly in view. Try to describe for yourself what the motive of each of the characters is. It is not difficult to do this if you think in terms of some infinitive. For example, the motive of Horner, plainly enough, is to deceive the town into believing he is a eunuch. Other things follow from this motive, such as his gaining access to certain ladies, but the motive, basically, is what counts dramatically. Now if you examine the motives of others in the play you'll find that very many of them have a similar motive to Horner's. They take action accordingly – Pinchwife in one way, by pretending his pretty wife is ugly or even diseased; Lady Fidget in another way by making a date with Horner and pretending it is a harmless encounter; Harcourt in yet another way, by falsely assuming the role of a priest and wrecking Alithea's marriage ceremony. Sir Jasper Fidget, Sparkish and Alithea all deceive themselves, in different ways. All of these motives combine and feed into the central action, dominated by Horner. The play, therefore, is a series of images of society, revealing how everybody is moving in the same direction, in search of love or pleasure or security but always engaged in deception.

You will see, then, that the play is a series of interlocking stories – Horner's, Pinchwife's, Alithea's, and so on, all forming patterns of cause and effect: the actions of one character affect the actions of another character, and so it goes on. To seize hold of the meaning of the play, you might chart out the various sub-plots, on a piece of paper, and connect them up, by appropriate lines, with the Horner story. Thus if Horner is placed in the centre of a circle and the men (Sir Jasper, Sparkish, Pinchwife, Harcourt) are on the periphery, the lines that can be drawn to suggest the action form a cobweb. Horner is at the centre like a clever spider, luring those who really should keep away but who end up feeding him in one way or another. The overall joke is that the spider, by declaring himself harmless, lets the anxiety or lust or sloth of others lead them into the web woven by deceit. The action reveals the springs of motivations in society, and these are laughably at variance with what people assert or even believe to be true.

The action of a comedy invariably leads to a clarification of what people really are or want from life. The plot of comedy builds from an absurd situation, such as Horner's scheme (in I.1), and then gets complicated as various mistakes occur. In *The Country Wife* the mistakes stem from Pinchwife's not realising that Horner is supposed to be impotent: eventually he brings his own wife to Horner by mistake. The complications which arise from Horner's managing to have several lovers without sharing his secret among them, lead to the climax of the action, when (in V.4) it looks as if Horner's whole scheme is about to involve him in one duel with Harcourt and another duel with Pinchwife, with Sir Jasper a prospect for a third. But this possibility is averted when society closes ranks to protect its own interests (which happen to coincide with Horner's interest). So clarification comes in this play not with the usual revelation of the truth, the establishment of true identities and so forth, but through Margery's education into the ways of the world. Once the country wife sees and accepts how a woman survives in city love affairs she agrees to shut her mouth. As a result, Pinchwife thinks he is being told the truth at last about Horner, and all's well that ends well. Comedy invariably ends in harmony, all confusion ended and all discords resolved. So it is in *The Country Wife*, but we have to notice that this is ironic. In other words, we do *not* get the sort of plot resolution and clarification usual to comedy, but instead are asked to approve of a cover-up which is supported by the majority on stage. This is ironic because it seems to be one thing (the revelation of truth) but is actually another (the establishment of deceit). And when we accept this with a smile we are acknowledging that society more often compromises the truth than resolutely lives by it. The comic action endorses social deceit.

Question: the structure, the handling of the three plots, of *The Country Wife* has been much admired. Can you say, in detail, why it is admirable?

The role of style

When reading and studying *The Country Wife* you must never forget that its main purpose is to give pleasure. It is not a play to be read for deep meanings: it doesn't have any. It has, instead, immense style. You must try to attune to this quality in the text, if your appreciation of its merits are to grow and take shape. In order to illuminate this area, a few comments are offered here, firstly on the nature of style in the society which the play records and secondly on Wycherley's use of prose style.

Style in society

Style is always difficult to define. We say a performer or a sportsman has style if he or she manages movements gracefully. We imply by this admiration that the performer has the power to order and control the body so as to create something beautiful. Style is an aesthetic principle, then; its possessor has a sense of beauty. But it also implies economy. A stylish performer doesn't waste effort; he or she makes all seem effortless.

If you transfer this simple notion of the stylish sportsperson to the larger scale of the social playground, what can you say about style? In society, what amounts to having and displaying style? We tend to think first of dress here, and to describe the stylish as those whose appearance is admirable and whose *manner* of displaying dress is beautiful. But, on reflection, we realise that taste is a significant feature of style in this sense. The wearer of beautiful clothes has to know *instinctively* how to combine colours, how to offset lines and bodily shape, how to create the best effect. This means that the stylish person has to have an innate quality or power, something like the power of an artist. He or she has to have a sense of design, and this is a dynamic, not a static quality. Therefore, when we talk about style we talk about somebody of talent acting upon and with certain materials.

It is possible to go a step further now and suggest that there is another and higher meaning of style. We don't usually mean, when we describe somebody as having style, that that person has it only for an occasion. We mean he or she has it as a constant quality. We mean, indeed, that he or she has a habit or mode of living which makes possible this consistent creation of a good impression: 'good', that is, in the sense of beautiful. Therefore we can consider style as a way of living, as a mode of shaping, ordering and controlling experience so as to create a pleasing effect on others. Style now becomes a philosophy, an ethic. What appears easy and effortless to admirers will have been the product of discipline and belief in a particular design for living. The poet W.B. Yeats (1865–1939) says in 'Adam's Curse', 'we must labour to be beautiful', but the labour must not be visible.

A society which elevates style as an ideal of conduct is, of necessity, secular. It is a society which ceases to look to God and to religion for its standards of behaviour. At its extreme, we call such a society 'decadent', a term often too loosely applied. Decadence means a decline, literally a falling away, from some high-point of achievement. It does not necessarily mean 'corrupt'. For example, it is common to describe the period of the eighteen-nineties as decadent, because it was a time when writers and artists pursued an ideal of 'art for art's sake', and moved away from realism towards symbolism. They 'fell away' from the straight-forward principles of Christian humanism and followed instead a gospel of the beautiful. Morally, this meant that orthodox standards for judging behaviour were replaced by standards of beauty. As Oscar Wilde (1854–1900) put it in his play, *The Importance of Being Earnest* (1895), 'In matters of grave importance, style, not sincerity, is the vital thing.' This attitude sums up what is meant by 'decadence'. It can be said, though this is something that might well be disputed, that a similar development took place during Restoration times. It was a time of decadence, inasmuch as it represented a falling away from the strict, Puritan ideals and principles which had governed English society during the Commonwealth period (1642–60).

What, then, is the role of style in *The Country Wife*? *The Country Wife* is a mirror: it reflects back the society of the day. This point is borne out by the testimony of the writer Sir Richard Steele (1672–1729) who said in his periodical *The Tatler* (No. 3, 1709) that *The Country Wife* was 'a good Representation of the Age in which that Comedy was written'. It was an age of dressing up. Men wore long wigs and painted their faces; women wore masks, and at times wore disguise (the Duchess of Cleveland, for example, disguised herself as a country girl when visiting Wycherley). You could say it was an age of pretence. Style meant having the wit, the intellectual power, to make the pretence seem real. Those lacking in wit, in discrimination, were excessive in their style, just as those who had wit knew instinctively how to strike a balance between nature, what is, and art, what might be. Sparkish, in the play, is lacking in wit and therefore in style. He habitually acts as if the world is looking at him, and he tries feverishly to meet its expectations. He is hollow, having no vital centre from which his actions can flow. He is all imitation, all falseness. Yet he often passes for the real thing, especially for Alithea, who is short-sighted in regard to his emptiness. Horner, however, sees him 'as a false jewel amongst true ones' (I.1.233–4), an image that says it all: Sparkish has only exterior style, not interior merit. He confesses: 'we wits rail and make love often but to show our parts [talents]; as we have no affections, so we have no malice' (II.1.257–9). That is to say, he and his like talk and make love only for show: it all means nothing and has no passion behind it. Wycherley maintains this is not style; this is ridiculous affectation. Affectation is the great enemy to style.

Those who are guilty of affectation in the play are all afraid of something, be it ridicule or exposure. Thus, Lady Fidget and her friends pretend to a modesty, a habitual decency, which is false; their role-playing is uneasy, however, as they constantly fear exposure and behave accordingly. Pinchwife so fears ridicule (and dispossession of his precious acquisition, Margery), that he has no sense of style at all. Sir Jasper Fidget is so preoccupied with his own convenience that he never questions or doubts Horner's affliction (and hence his wife's fidelity), as if he dare not know the truth, which would destroy his comfortable arrangements. So, Sir Jasper is a fool, whose design for living is bereft of human understanding. On the other hand Margery, Alithea, Harcourt and Horner all take risks. All live dangerously, to some extent, and go against the narrow rules laid down by people like Pinchwife. The style they display is thus an expression of their inner selves. It has a certain recklessness about it that tells us they are fully alive. It is this quality that the play celebrates, genuine style rather than hollow affectation.

Wycherley's prose style

Restoration comedy, in general, is remarkable for its fine prose. Dryden, a playwright himself, said that all the writers had to do was to listen to the good conversation at the court of Charles II, and learn how to reproduce it, so high was its standard of wit and polish. The plays, then, imitated life in this respect also, that they captured the actual grace of real conversation.

In drama, prose is always the sign of realism, whereas verse attempts something beyond realism, something lyrical or poetic. Wycherley's prose does not achieve the heights of Congreve's, which is probably the best of the age, but nevertheless it has that classical, clear quality which Congreve refined upon until he created a language at once perfectly natural and very beautiful.

One of the tricks or strategies Wycherley uses in dialogue is to exploit decorum. Decorum means making a character speak as he might be expected to in real life. But since Wycherley is a satirist, he likes to let one character pick up, as it were, the phrases used by another and repeat them ironically. The effect is that the attention of the audience is drawn to the language, as a means of measuring intentions or intelligence. For example, when Horner secretly tells Lady Fidget that he is not, in fact, impotent, she asks, 'But, indeed, sir, as perfectly, perfectly, the same man as before going into France, sir? As perfectly, perfectly, sir?' (II.1.527–8). Her anxiety is comic: she *wants* him to be lusty, a strange concern for a supposed virtuous, married woman! Horner's reply, reassuring her, mimics her language: 'As perfectly, perfectly, madam' (line 529). When Harcourt tries to persuade Sparkish to speak to Alithea, so that he himself can court her, the contest between them is registered in language that again uses repetition – this time with more subtle ironic undertones. There is also use of antithesis (or contrast) and of balance:

HARCOURT: Come, Sparkish, your mistress saw you, and will be angry you go not to her. Besides, I would fain [like to] be reconciled to her, which none but you can do, *dear friend*.

SPARKISH: Well, that's a better reason, *dear friend*. I would not go near her now, for hers or my own sake, but I can deny you nothing; for though I have known thee a great while, never go, if I do not love thee as well as a new acquaintance.

HARCOURT: I am obliged to you indeed, *dear friend*. I would be well with her, only to be well with thee still; for these ties to wives usually dissolve all ties to friends. I would be contented she should enjoy you *a-nights*, but I would have you to myself *a-days*, as I have had, *dear friend*.

SPARKISH: And thou shalt enjoy me a-days, *dear, dear friend*, never stir [fear]; and I'll be divorced from *her*, sooner than from *thee*.

(III.2.159–72, my italics)

Here, the repetition of 'dear friend' when it is clear to the audience that Harcourt is insincere, serves to reveal the nature of friendship in this society. The tone, on Harcourt's part, is ironic, though he has to be careful. There is also use of antithesis, as in 'a-nights . . . a-days' and balance, as in 'her . . . thee'. This neat ordering of the language, if carefully studied (look again at the repetition all through Harcourt's last speech here), beautifully reveals the hollowness of friendship.

You might like to explore another passage for yourself. The exchange between Lady Fidget and Horner in the 'drinking' scene (V.4. 72–95) offers an excellent example of Wycherley's prose style. Why can it be said that this passage is ironic in the extreme?

One way of attending to Wycherley's style, finally, is to bear in mind all the time that he is writing satire, that he is criticising the manners he is realistically displaying. We are meant, as it were, to *overhear* the exchanges between characters, and to see in them a kind of competition which will make certain key words stand out in a new light.

Acting the play

Reading the text of a play is a very poor substitute for seeing it on stage. *The Country Wife* is full of invitations to the actors and actresses as to how they might act out their roles. It is not so easy to see these 'invitations' by simply reading the words silently on a page. For example, take the passage just quoted at length, between Sparkish and Harcourt. It calls for an understanding between the two actors. Harcourt must be slightly sneering, but not too much; Sparkish must be eager to please, but believable. An adjustment of voices is called for. Much of the fun in the play comes from this sort of close playing together – *as if* each actor did not know what the other was at, whereas, in fact, of course, he does.

If it is possible for you to read *The Country Wife* in company with others you will find its comic undertones become much more obvious. Better still, if a few of your friends will agree to read a few scenes and take roles you will be surprised at the difference this can make to your understanding of the play. Take, for example, a fairly simple scene, in I.1, where Pinchwife is teased about his wife by Horner, Harcourt and Dorilant. He has got to 'play up' so as to give them something to act against: he must appear jealous, suspicious, foolishly secretive, while they, in varying ways, keep stalking him, possibly following him around the stage, as they try to get him to admit he has married a pretty wife. The scene, as does the play as a whole, calls for naturalistic acting with just a degree of over-playing, for it is only if the performers exaggerate slightly that the farcical side of certain scenes will emerge. Likewise with the scenes that call for expert timing – the 'china' scene or the great final scene – to read these aloud with an attempt at staying in character, is to begin to appreciate Wycherley's comic technique. Much fun can be gained from such dramatic readings and they serve to remind us that the play is, after all, only make-believe, calling for the skills of performers to make its laughable qualities resoundingly clear. *The Country Wife* is first and foremost entertainment, and even though it demands talents of a high order in performance and requires bright costumes and changeable scenery, a step towards appreciating its entertainment-value can be made by even the simplest prepared reading.

Some sample questions and model answers

'The triumph of true wit over foppery is an essential theme in *The Country Wife*.' Discuss.

The Country Wife is a satiric comedy. It is concerned with exposing certain faults and failings in polite society. One such failing is the pretence to wit.

Wit is a difficult concept to define. Clearly enough, it has to do with a linguistic ability to express thoughts in a way that causes surprise and induces laughter. In Restoration comedy everybody seems expected to possess wit. It is a competitive society that is depicted, and part of the competition is expressed through words. When characters meet they usually fence with words and in the course of that verbal contest they display quickness of mind. This is always the case with the lovers, who at first seem only to be fighting with each other but who are, in fact, taking delight in each other's ability to return a sharp sally of wit. In *The Country Wife* true wit is revealed when Harcourt and Alithea meet for the first time (II.1). He falls in love with her at first sight, but because she is engaged to be married to Sparkish he must pretend only to be chatting to his friend's girl-friend. He has, therefore, to exercise his intelligence in order to pay compliments to Alithea while not arousing the suspicion of Sparkish. She, for her part, although attracted to Harcourt, finds it necessary to repel his advances because she is loyal to Sparkish. Therefore her response to Harcourt takes the form of turning back his compliments. Their conversation is thus a kind of game, between two lively and intelligent people.

An example of this kind of repartee occurs when Alithea tells Harcourt that Sparkish must love her or he would not marry her, and he replies: 'Marrying you is no more sign of his love, than bribing your woman [servant], that he may marry you, is a sign of his generosity . . . But if you take marriage for a sign of love, take it from me immediately' (II.1.218–23). Later on (in III.2), when Alithea tries to show Sparkish that Harcourt is abusing his friendship by courting her, we get further evidence of Harcourt's wit, as he evades observation and continues to pay compliments to Alithea. There is a contest going on here not so much between Harcourt and Alithea as between true wit and foppery, with Sparkish as the fop.

Sparkish likes to think he is a wit but he is, in fact, a fool. Before he comes on stage at all he is described by those who know him, Horner, Harcourt and Dorilant, as a mere pretender to wit. Horner says he is a nuisance because he never understands the conversation he insists on butting in on. Also, by trying too hard to be a wit he is actually the opposite, 'the greatest fop, dullest ass, and worst company' (I.1.261–2). When Sparkish comes in we see how true this is. He tries all the time to impress but the harder he tries the less effective he is. After this, in the scenes where Harcourt woos Alithea before his very eyes, he is revealed as very stupid. He can't see what is going on, how he is being fooled by Harcourt. A man of wit should be a man of intelligence, but Sparkish has very little intelligence. He likes to be thought of as clever, however, and the only time he feels insulted is when he thinks Harcourt has suggested he has no talents ('parts') of that kind. Because he regards himself as a man-about-town, in the height of fashion, Sparkish is constantly running off to some important social engagement or other, to the king's court at Whitehall or to the theatre. It is made clear that he goes to such places only to be seen. He contributes nothing, but rather is a source of laughter because of his silly behaviour. When he describes how he behaves at the theatre we realise that he is more a loudmouth than a wit: 'the reason why we are so often louder than the players is because we think we speak more wit, and so become the poet's rivals in his audience' (III.2.91–3). Little does he seem to know what a typical public nuisance he must be!

In this love triangle, Harcourt continues to win over Sparkish and in the end gets the hand of Alithea in marriage. Harcourt displays his wit in this victory when, by dressing up as a parson, he easily pulls the wool over Sparkish's eyes and ensures that Sparkish's marriage doesn't take place. In the end, therefore, it is quite true that true wit triumphs over foppery, or vanity. The triumph is signified by the marriage of Alithea and Harcourt.

This is indeed an essential theme of the play as a whole because in other areas, such as Horner's outwitting of Sir Jasper Fidget and of Pinchwife, we can see a similar sort of victory of inventiveness and quickness over pretentiousness and dullness. In the sort of comedy which *The Country Wife* is, it is not so much a case of true love conquering all as it is of true wit conquering all.

'The main force of Wycherley's satire is directed against female hypocrisy.' Discuss.

Horner's friend, Quack, who has spread the story around town that Horner is a eunuch, finds it difficult to understand how the story will benefit Horner. The latter explains. A man's greatest problem is to know which women would be interested in an affair and which would not: 'But now I can be sure she that shows an aversion to me loves the sport' (I.1.151−2). Also, he goes on, his plot will provide a screen for those women who *are* interested, because they are worried only about protecting their 'reputations, not their persons' (line 155) from the breath of scandal. This revelation prepares us for the possibility that the women in the play will prove Horner right. If they do, then clearly his cynical assessment will have established their hypocrisy.

Lady Fidget behaves exactly as Horner has predicted. At first she displays disgust at Horner's condition and wants nothing to do with him. Psychologically, this implies a desire for the contrary, a man who would *not* be a eunuch. But she masks this sexual desire under the appearance of extreme delicacy. Indeed she tries to give the impression that the very mention of sex or even of the word 'naked' is too shocking for her to allow. At one point she even insists on leaving a room just because Pinchwife has entered: 'O lord, here's a man! Sir Jasper, my mask, my mask! I would not be seen here for the world' (IV.3.228−9). 'Here' is in fact Horner's lodgings, where she has just had sex with Horner. Yet she pretends to be so modest that she couldn't afford even to be *seen* in the place. She usually supports her claim to modesty by talking much about her 'honour', meaning her virtue, or so we think at first. But when she is attracted to Horner, after he tells her his secret, she harps so much on her 'honour', which he must protect, that we know she cannot mean her virtue. It is *she* who would have to protect her honour, by staying away from Horner; therefore what she is asking him to do is simply to ensure that nobody finds out about their adultery: 'you must promise to have a care of my dear honour' (IV.3.41–2). It is plain, then, that she is a hypocrite, and that Horner was right. Later in the play, in the 'drinking' scene, she openly confesses to Horner that her insistence on honour was only a means of protecting her good name.

Lady Fidget's companions, Mrs Dainty Fidget and Mrs Squeamish, behave in exactly the same way. In the 'china' scene they display a comical eagerness to have a share of Horner's 'china', while at the same time they pretend that they are interested in Horner only as a slavish companion. Like Lady Fidget they too know Horner's secret and flock to him accordingly. Under the influence of drink, later on, they too reveal 'the truth of our hearts' (V.4.20), and this truth exposes their hypocrisy.

Horner, of course, enjoys the pleasure of being right about these women in more senses than one. This is where satire comes into the picture. It is the playwright who makes use of Horner in order to show to us the double standards by which the women of the age lived. This satire is not directed against Alithea or against Margery, the country wife. Alithea is not a hypocrite, and is never in the least attracted towards Horner. Margery *is* attracted, but not because she hears the story of his impotence: she does *not* hear it, indeed, and this is one of the ironies of the play. Margery is so far from being a hypocite that she almost brings ruin on Horner in the end by attempting to blurt out, as if in his defence, the news that he is not at all impotent. But this naïveté probably underlines all the more firmly the hypocrisy of Lady Fidget and her friends. After all, Margery never talks about her honour. She wants only love, and goes about finding it in as direct a way as her animal nature and jealous husband instruct. Therefore, it is certainly valid to claim that the main force of Wycherley's satire is directed against female hypocrisy.

Part 5

Suggestions for further reading

The text

William Wycherley: The Country Wife, edited by John Dixon Hunt, The New Mermaids, Ernest Benn, London, 1973. (Reprinted A. & C. Black, London, 1985.) Line references in these Notes are to this edition.

William Wycherley: The Country Wife, edited by David Cook and John Swannell. The Revels Plays, Methuen, London, 1975. This is an excellent edition, now unfortunately out of print, with a very full introduction and useful notes.

Three Restoration Comedies, edited by Gamini Salgado, Penguin Books, Harmondsworth, 1968. This contains *The Country Wife*, together with Etherege's *The Man of Mode* and Congreve's *Love for Love*. It has a good introduction, which gives a wide and lively account of Restoration comedy.

The Dramatic Works of Wycherley, Congreve, Vanbrugh and Farquhar, edited by Leigh Hunt, Routledge, London, 1840. An out-of-print book to be looked up in the library. It has interesting introductions.

Restoration Comedy, edited by A. Norman Jeffares, Folio Press, London/Rowman & Littlefield, Totowa, New Jersey, 1974. Volume I of this four-volume edition contains *The Country Wife*.

The Plays of William Wycherley, edited by Arthur Friedman, Clarendon Press, Oxford, 1979.

General reading

BIRDSALL, VIRGINIA OGDEN: *Wild Civility: The English Comic Spirit on the Restoration Stage*, Indiana University Press, Bloomington & London, 1970. A lively book with a chapter on *The Country Wife*.

CHADWICK, W.R.: *The Four Plays of William Wycherley*, Mouton, The Hague, 1975. Has a good chapter on *The Country Wife*.

DOBRÉE, BONAMY: *Restoration Comedy 1660–1720*, Oxford University

Press, Oxford, 1924. A standard critical work, often reprinted. It has a chapter on Wycherley.

HUME, ROBERT D: *The Development of English Drama in the Late Seventeenth Century*, Clarendon Press, Oxford, 1976. A scholarly book, for the advanced student.

HOLLAND, NORMAN: *The First Modern Comedies*, Harvard University Press, Cambridge (Mass.), 1959. A very stimulating book on Restoration comedy.

HOLLAND, PETER: *The Ornament of Action: Text and Performance in Restoration Comedy*, Cambridge University Press, Cambridge, 1979. For the advanced student, this book has a lot of detail on staging matters.

KRUTCH, JOSEPH WOOD: *Comedy and Conscience after the Restoration*, Columbia University Press, 1924, 1949, paperback 1961. Like Dobrée's study, above, this book is a standard work.

MUIR, KENNETH: *The Comedy of Manners*, Hutchinson University Library, London, 1970. A study of Restoration comedy, with a chapter on Wycherley. A good book to start with.

POWELL, JOCELYN: *Restoration Theatre Production*, Routledge and Kegan Paul, London, 1984. Deals, as the title implies, with the theatrical rather than the literary qualities. It has a chapter on *The Country Wife*.

RIGHTER, ANNE: 'William Wycherley', in *Restoration Theatre*, edited by John Russell Brown and Bernard Harris, Edward Arnold, London, 1965. A wide-ranging survey of all of his plays.

ZIMBARDO, ROSE A.: *Wycherley's Drama*, Yale University Press, New Haven and London, 1965. A thorough examination of Wycherley as satirist.

The author of these notes

CHRISTOPHER MURRAY is a Statutory Lecturer in the Department of English at University College, Dublin. He was educated at University College, Galway, and Yale University. His publications include an edition of an Irish Restoration comedy, *St Stephen's Green*, by William Philips (1980), and a study of the Regency theatre, *Robert William Elliston, Manager* (1975). In 1983 his *Selected Plays of Lennox Robinson* appeared. He acted as secretary of the International Association for the Study of Anglo-Irish Literature (IASAIL) from 1973 to 1976 and edited its *Newsletter*. A member of the executive board of *Irish University Review* since 1977, he was its guest editor for the commemorative issue on Sean O'Casey, in spring 1980. He is also author of York Notes on Marlowe's *Doctor Faustus* and Marlowe's *Edward II*.